The Penguin Book of

B	A	R	N	R	A	M	P	S
B	O	R	N	V	A	M	P	S
W	O	R	N	G	A	M	P	S
W	O	R	D	G	A	M	E	S
W	O	L	D	N	A	M	E	S
C	O	L	D	D	A	M	E	S
B	O	L	D	D	A	T	E	S
B	A	L	D	P	A	T	E	S

David Parlett

Penguin Books

Penguin Books Ltd, Harmondsworth, Middlesex, England
Penguin Books, 625 Madison Avenue, New York, New York 10022, U.S.A.
Penguin Books Australia Ltd, Ringwood, Victoria, Australia
Penguin Books Canada Ltd, 2801 John Street, Markham, Ontario, Canada L3R 1B4
Penguin Books (N.Z.) Ltd, 182-190 Wairau Road, Auckland 10, New Zealand

First published 1982

Photoset in Linocomp Times by
Rowland Phototypesetting Ltd, Bury St Edmunds, Suffolk
Made and printed in Great Britain by
Cox & Wyman Ltd, Reading

Penguin Books
The Penguin Book of Word Games

Born in London and bred in Wales, David Parlett was a
language teacher, technical writer and public relations
practitioner before becoming a freelance journalist/author
specializing in games. He is the inventor of several published
games, including *Hare and Tortoise* and *Pot Black Snooker
Dice*, and of some original card games, such as *Ninety-nine*,
which has claimed many addicts in the Bridge world. He is a
consultant editor to *The Gamer* (formerly *Games & Puzzles*)
magazine, to which he contributed a monthly column
entitled *On the Cards* for several years. Besides two books
on linguistic subjects, he is the author of *Original Card
Games, Card Games for Two, Card Games for Three, Card
Games for Four* and *Know the Game: Patience*. David
Parlett is married, has two children and lives in South
London.

He is also the author of *The Penguin Book of Card Games*
and *The Penguin Book of Patience*.

to Len and Isa Mitchell

Contents

Fun and Wordgames   11

    Part One: *Spoken Word Games*

1 *Pundemonium*   15

Knock, Knock, Who's There?–What Sort of Game am I?–The Game of the Name–Daft Definitions–Orrible Origins–Silly Similes–Vulture Up To?–Tonto–Tom Swifties–Defective Detective

2 *Performances*   27

Teapot–Bananas–Hobby Horse–Quick Thinking–Inquisition–Adverbs–The Railway Carriage Game–Just a Minute–Ad Lib–Yessir, Nossir–Taboo–Spelling Bee–Spelling Round

3 *Proverbials*   42

Proverbs–Shouting Proverbs–Dumb Crambo–Charades

4 *Alphabeticals*   50

I Love My Love–The Travelling Alphabet–The A-to-Z Banquet–Hypochondriac–I Packed My Bag–Oral Alphabent

5 *Sequentials*   55

Buzz, Bizz and Roman Buzz–The Tennis-Elbow-Foot Game–Free Association–Mornington Crescent–Heads and Tails–Trailers–Crambo–Life Sentence–Acronymia–Up the Dictionary

6 *Ghostlies*   64

Ghost–Superghost–Anaghost–Ultraghost

7   *Deductives*   70

I Spy–Key Word–Twenty Questions–Who Am I?–
Botticelli–Backenforth–Clue Words–Shaffe's Game–
Aesop's Mission–Kolodny's Game

Part Two: *Written Word Games*

8   *Compilations*   85

Digrams–Trigrams–Prefixes–Suffixes–Fore and Aft–
Head to Tail–Bacronyms–Sequences–Stairway–
Beheadings–Numwords–Categories and Guggenheim–
Word Ladders

9   *In-words*   99

Word Hunt–Acrosticals–Name in Vain

10   *Sequentials*   105

Uncrash–Word Ping-Pong–Nymphabet–Arrow of
Letters–Centurion–Inflation–Oilers

11   *Narratives*   119

Telegrams–Alphabent–Constructapo–Consequences–
Headlines–Pass It On

12   *Cross Words*   129

Double Cross–Alphacross–Scramble–Sinko–
Wordsworth–Lynx–Pi–Black Squares–Ragaman–Last
Word

13   *Fictionaries*   162

Fictionary Dictionary–Fabulary Vocabulary–
Encyclopedia Fictannica–Whose Who's Who?–Blind
Dates–Captions Courageous–Suspended Sentences

14   *Deductives*   178

Anagrams–Hangman–Jotto–Double Jeopardy–Crash–
Wild Crash–Convergence–Quizl–Get the Message–
Foreheads

Postscripts

Acceptability of words in word games	197
Some useful statistics for word-gamers	223
Solutions to problems	227
Bibliography	230
Index of games	233

Acknowledgements

My thanks are due to David Pritchard, editor of *The Gamer* (formerly *Games & Puzzles*), for permission to re-use games of mine and others first published in the magazine; to Gyles Brandreth for permission to use games of his invention and for information on rules followed by the British National Scrabble Championship; to Matthew Reisz of Penguin Books for stimulating discussion on many points and for improving some of my examples; and to the Estate of Sir Arnold Bax for permission to reproduce an extract from the composer's poetry.

Fun and Wordgames

Playing with words is a pleasure to which I am as addicted as anyone. Unlike most addictions, it has not yet been shown by scientists to harden the arteries or by evangelists to threaten perdition, so with any luck it is probably here to stay.

There are good reasons for the popularity of word games.

For one thing, *word games are free*, like all the best things in life. Few call for anything costlier than pencil and paper; many dispense even with these.

Again, *word games require no specialized knowledge*. You can't learn Bridge without lengthy initiation into the mysteries of tricks and trumps and signalling systems, or Chess without going at some length into standard openings and common, endgame positions. But anyone with an average English vocabulary has some fifteen to twenty thousand gaming units at their disposal, complete with elaborate rules of movement, which they practise day after day without a moment's hesitation.

Best of all, *word games are more imaginative than other games*. Chess relates to nothing outside its monotonous universe of black and white, and if cards are prettier, they are still essentially abstract. Only in word games can you pass camels with ease through the eye of a needle, or transmute NAPOLEON into ANN POOLE at the stroke of a pen.

More serious recommendations can be found, if you want them. In the wrong hands (or mouths) words can be dangerous – remember Newspeak in Orwell's *1984* – or lure the unwary into making fools of themselves – see the 'Ongoing Situations' column or 'Pseuds' Corner' in the magazine *Private Eye*. (And how many sociologists might envy the character of Jane

Austen's who 'cannot speak well enough to be unintelligible'!) Of all people, the habitual word-gamer is perhaps best equipped to resist the more sinister wordplay of everyday propagandists, be they advertisers, loonie sects or so-called liberation movements.

Or politicians. But there may be hope for them. The *Guardian* recently revealed details of a word game popular in the House of Commons. Players from all parties agree on some unusual word – such as *scrunt* – and the winner is the first person to get it published in *Hansard* under their own name. Such people can't all be bad. I bet they don't play anything like that in the Kremlin.

For them, and you (and me), I have sought to gather most of the world's best word games together in this book. Some have been passed on by word of mouth, some stolen from other people's books, and one or two invented by myself. (Sources are credited where known, and I apologize to anyone who may feel left out.) Part One describes word games played orally – not to say loudly, many of them being party games suitable for children and intelligent adults. Part Two deals with pencil-and-paper games, which generally require more thinking. All are fun, and most are competitive, in that points may be scored and someone declared a winner. Because some people think this important, I have sometimes suggested scoring systems for games which previously worked quite well without them. These, however, can be treated as optional. In my view, winning is only the *object* of a game, not its *purpose*.

Each game in the book is prefaced with a threefold note. The first gives an estimate as to how many may play it. The second suggests a suitable age for them to be at the time. The third distinguishes a serious from a light-hearted game, or at least recommends a frame of mind in which to approach it.

If you don't agree with any of the rules, change them; and if you don't like any of the jokes, send me some better ones.

Part One
Spoken Word Games

The other project was a scheme for entirely abolishing all words whatsoever; and this was urged as a great advantage in point of health, as well as brevity. For it is plain, that every word we speak is, in some degree, a diminution of our lungs by corrosion; and consequently contributes to the shortening of our lives.

SWIFT, *Gulliver's Travels*

1 · *Pundemonium*

or Pun is from Heaven

The third is its slowness in taking a jest.
    Should you happen to venture on one
It will sigh like a thing that is deeply distressed:
    And it always looks grave at a pun.

LEWIS CARROLL, *The Hunting of the Snark*

The pun is often defined as a 'play on words', but as this applies to almost anything from Spoonerisms to Eskimo Nell it doesn't get us very far. More precisely, it is an ambiguous word, deliberately chosen for humorous effect, which is approached in one sense and quitted in another, thus leading the listener up the proverbial garden path. Thomas Hood, the punster's poet, illustrates it admirably with:

They went and told the sexton, and
the sexton tolled the bell.

The point at which the listener is misled up the garden path can be shown by overlapping the two sense-directions like this:

. . . the sexton told . . .
        . . . tolled the bell.

(It works less well on the reader, who is forewarned by the spelling.)

Puns are unjustly despised. The 'correct' response to one is conventionally a groan instead of a laugh. Such contempt is not new: the mealy-mouthed Joseph Addison (1672–1719) is said to have dismissed the pun as 'the lowest form of wit'. ('Yes,' countered a keener mind, 'because it is the foundation of all wit.')

Why should this be? Perhaps because the most witless of people can spot word resemblances and draw attention to them, with the result that most puns of everyday occurrence are not worth hearing. A good pun must be based on a single word, or at least on two so similar as to resemble one; but even this is not enough. The point of a pun is that its two meanings should also bear some sensible relationship to each other. It is because so few everyday puns fulfil either requirement that even the good pun, when it does occur, tends to find itself tarred with the same brush-off.

Another possible explanation is simply that people don't like being taken by surprise. Just as a groan may be accepted as the 'correct' response to a poke in the ribs, may it not also be regarded as an equally correct response to a poke in the wits?

I like puns. To me, they are not only the foundation but also the punnacle of wit. By way of celebration, not to say indulgence, I will open these proceedings with a veritable Pundora's Box of word games entirely based on this exquisite torture.

Knock, Knock, Who's There?

Any number of players
Any age
Fun rather than competitive

A: Knock, knock!
Q: Who's there?
A: Mary.
Q: Mary who?
A: Mary Christmas and a Happy New Year.

Jokes tend to go in phases. Remember elephant jokes? 'How does an elephant camouflage himself? By painting the soles of his feet yellow and floating upside-down in a bowl of custard.' And Irish jokes? 'What's black and crisp and hangs upside-down from the ceiling? An Irish electrician.'

Knock, knock jokes all follow the pattern illustrated above and will probably last forever, since one of their attractions is audience participation. In our circle all conversation is politely broken off when somebody, after looking thoughtful for a few moments, interposes a decisive 'Knock, knock!'; it would be considered the height of rudeness not to respond.

Q: Who's there?
A: Don Giovanni.
Q: Don Giovanni who?
A: Don Giovann' any ice cream today?

The knocker is usually given a genuine name, but there are some nonsense classics in the repertoire. Imagine the stunned silence which must have greeted this one when it first came out (and is probably, I'm afraid, still the reaction of American readers unacquainted with the delivery considered appropriate to slush songs in England):

Q: Who's there?
A: M. A. B. It's a big horse.
Q: M. A. B. It's a big horse who?
A (*sings*): M. A. B. It's a big horse I'm a Londoner/That I love London Town . . .

This pun looks phonetically excruciating at first, though careful examination shows that it is a perfect reproduction of the phrase 'Maybe it's because' as sung in the style referred to.

Punchlines that have to be sung to make their point are always good for an extra laugh. This one uses an almost genuine name:

Q: Who's there?
A: Armelline.
Q: Armelline who?
A: Armellinin' on a lamp-post at the corner of the street/In case a certain little lady comes by.

Of course, if you rhyme her with 'shine' instead of 'sheen', you're lost.

A peculiar variation on the theme occurs in the following rather erudite encounter:

Q: Who's there?
A: Sutton
Q: Sutton who?
A: Burial chamber.

To play this as a game, seat everybody in the inevitable circle (or evitable square, or some such topological equivalent) and decide who goes first and the order of play. Each player in turn must produce a Knock, knock riddle that has not already been used in the same game, though, of course, one doesn't expect everyone to come up with brand new ones on the spur of the moment. Whoever fails to have one ready at his turn to play drops out (forfeits optional); the winner is the last left in.

A more interesting way of playing is as follows:

Arnold Knock, knock!
Byron Who's there?
Coleridge Dolores.
Dickens Dolores who?
Eliot [George, not T.S.] Er . . . um . . .
Fitzgerald Um . . . er . . .
Gaskell (sings) Dolores be an England/And England shall be free . . .

Eliot and Fitzgerald have certainly lost and have to pay forfeits, e.g. Eliot to sing something basso profundo and Fitzgerald to recite the whole of the *Ruba'iyat* backwards. Mrs Gaskell has won only if she escapes with her life.

What Sort of Game am I?

Any number of players
Mainly for children
Fun rather than competitive

My family employs this as an in-car game. It drives me to

distraction. Something of its flavour may be got from the following example:

> *Arnold* I'm a key. What sort of key am I?
> *Byron* A don-key? (No.)
> *Eliot* A tur-key? (Ditto.)
> *Byron* A door key? (Negative.)
> *Gaskell* A flun-key? (Likewise.)
> *Coleridge* A Russ-ki? (Never.)
> *Dickens* Arthur As-key? . . .

. . . and so on, not necessarily playing in turn. Eventually one of them will get the right answer and take over the quiz-master's role. There is no need for the punning word to come at the end of the compound – the answer to this one could just as well turn out to be a key-schlorain, normally spelt *quiche lorraine*. Often, however, the players get so exasperated that they insist on being told whether the punned word comes first or last in the answer.

Be very careful when playing with young children who haven't yet got the hang of puns. Young Edward at his first attempt declared himself to be some kind of bus. We tried all sorts of buses, some of which he'd never heard of, such as arquebus, rebus and the like. Eventually we had to give up, only to discover that he was a 137 bus, having chosen a bus route with a high number so that we would take longer to get to it by following the most logical approach.

What Sort of Game am I? has a regrettable tendency to get silly as time passes, as witness the following:

> *Dickens* I'm a bit. What sort of bit am I?
> *Fitzgerald* A rab-bit?
> *Gaskell* A bit-tern?
> *Byron* A gam-bit?
> *All* Give up.
> *Dickens* I'm a bit fed up with this game. Let's play something else.

The Game of the Name

Any number of players
Any age
Fun rather than competitive

I can remember when the pinnacle of wit was reached by
reference to a book entitled 'Feeling Hungry' by Nora Bone.
Or 'Nearly Didn't Get Here at All' by Justin Thyme. Or
'That's Your Lot' by Maxie Mumm.

Even more popular than book titles as an excuse for
inventing a punny name are occupations. A recent issue of *The
Logophile* magazine carries a mass of additions to the genre,
showing what a long way we have come since children's comics
depicted all dental surgeries as sporting the nameplate
I. PULLEM – DENTIST. There are grocers called P. Green,
truckers called Laurie Driver and bandleaders called Tim
Panally. Ida Down is reported to have taken up quilt-making
and Evan Jellicle to have embraced Holy Orders. My own researches in this field have thrown up an unfulfilled boy wonder
called Peter Doubt, a Swedish dietician named Einar Fungry
and a decrepit Indian scrap-dealer known as Ram Shackle.

Ranks and titles can be commandeered to similar effect. The
army can boast among its personnel such names as Major
Breakthrough, Private Property and General Lee Speaking,
while the navy sails on in the capable hands of Abel Seeman
and your humble servant, Cap'n Hand.

You can turn this sort of thing into a game by simply
requiring each person in turn to quote a book title, occupation,
rank or whatever and leaving the name to be guessed, deduced
or dredged up from the depths of one's childhood memories.
Anyone who fails to have one ready when his turn comes
round loses a point – or a pound of flesh or whatever is agreed
on beforehand – and anyone who comes up with the correct
answer scores a point. (If all shout at once, they all score.) If
nobody guesses the correct name within a suitable period of
time, say three weeks, an extra point is scored by the player
who set the trap.

Since any one of these names can be used as the punchline of a Knock, knock (pp. 16–18), the two games should probably be lumped together as one.

Daft Definitions

Any number of players
Any age
Fun rather than competitive

The rawest type of pun derives from inventing homonymous definitions for words that lend themselves to the exercise, such as:

ALDERMEN = every male you can think of

BATTERY = place where bats live

CENTIMETRE = what you get when your wife's sister is due to arrive late at the station

DEHYDRATE = proportional excess tax you are charged for concealing your true income

EQUIPMENT = he was only joking

FAVOURABLE = prefer the male of the species

GLADIATOR = how the cannibal felt about his mother-in-law

And so on.

This is not so much a game as a habit. However, you could assign a letter of the alphabet to each player, with the instruction to think of a daft definition for a word beginning with it. The first to do so scores as many points as there are players, the second scores one less and so on, the game being played over as many rounds as agreed. Alternatively, the winner of each round is the player whose effort is voted the funniest or most ingenious.

Orrible Origins

A small number of players
Mainly for adults
Fun rather than competitive, but not easy

Listeners to BBC radio must be aware of the long-running game 'My Word', at whose climax Frank Muir and Denis Norden liven the whole thing up by revealing highly unlikely (but plausible) origins for well-known phrases, sayings or titles. I don't know if they invented the game, but they have certainly made it their own: some of their gems of invention have already been gathered together and published in book form.

For those who are unacquainted with what I call Orrible Origins I ought to give some genuine Muirish or Nordenian examples. Unfortunately, as always happens in these cases, I can't lay my hands on the book and the only one I can bring to mind is that which provided a title for it. One of the pair, asked to account for the well-known but, strictly speaking, meaningless phrase 'You can't have your cake and eat it', launched into some story about an Eskimo, presumably with bad circulation, who came to a nasty end by trying to warm his boat with a paraffin stove. All of which went to show that 'You can't have your kayak and heat it.'

As a matter of fact, I suspect that the phrase is often used when 'You can't have two bites at the cherry' would be more appropriate. This phrase, you may like to know, derives from the case of the harbourmaster who would not permit ships to dock until the captain had promised to treat him to a drink – as indicated by the message set up in naval flags over his office: 'You can't heave to – buy us a sherry.'

Or, to revert to a pun already quoted, the origin of a certain chauvinistic song may be traced back to a response recorded to the following taped message played to everyone entering the new, automated Blackwall Tunnel: 'When the pips sound, state the first three letters of your license plate, your means of transport and the place you come from.'

Whence 'M.A.B. It's a big horse. I'm a Londoner.'

How may Orrible Origins be turned into a formal game? Good question. Let me know when you think of an answer.

Silly Similes

Any number of players
Mainly for adults
Fun rather than competitive

An early Peter Sellers record entitled 'Balham – Gateway to the South' (a mock travelogue about an area of London where, as it happens, I used to go to school) contains a perversion of the line 'A rose-red city, half as old as time' into 'A rose-red city, half as gold as green'. Which, I suppose, will be lost on readers unaware that North London boasts an area blessed with the highly evocative name Golders Green.

Never mind. With the point of the pun revealed, the idea of the silly simile will be easily grasped from the following examples:

As right as cramp
As full as earth
As prime as stove
As foul as *Modern English Usage* . . .

. . . and so on.

A word-gaming friend and myself, working at them on and off, took about twenty years to extend this list to embrace about twenty examples. I then introduced them to readers of *Games & Puzzles* magazine and subsequently *The Logophile* in the form of a challenge to double the list. The response to both was extraordinarily enthusiastic. One writer had the effrontery to compile a list numbering three hundred plus, but I regret to say that many had to be disqualified for one reason or another. For instance, a basic requirement of the exercise is that the words on either side of the second 'as' should make sense. The district of Potters Bar would therefore not be accepted in the form 'as pot as bar', since there is no such adjective as 'pot'.

Reluctantly, I resist the temptation to list the fifty or so best examples of the silly simile yielded by both competitions. It will surely be more fun to think of them yourself, in the form of a game which is 'won' by the player who invents the most.

Vulture Up To?

Any number of players
Mainly for adults
Fun rather than competitive

This punning game was set as a competition by *Time* magazine in 1970 – or so I learn from Willard Espy's *Game of Words*, as I wasn't myself subscribing at the time. It seems to have started with punsters turning animal names into almost well-known phrases and sayings, such as:

OSTRICH in time saves nine
AARDVARK and no play makes Jack a dull boy
BUTTERFLY or I'll be late for dinner
WOODPECKER if she'd only let me
SEA ANEMONE, shoot on sight

Vulture Up To? works quite well as a party game if you can get people to think of (or, better still, come prepared with) suitable clues to which the pun is an answer. Award points or prizes for either divining the answer to someone else's clue or providing a clue to which nobody guesses the answer. For example: provide names for –

Marsupial fond of fizzy drinks (COCA KOALA)
Aquatic bird who always repays favours (ONE GOOD TERN)
Member of cat family who beats his cubs with open paw
(CUFF LYNX)

Tonto

Any number of players
Mainly for adults
Fun but skill-demanding

One of several games in this book reported as having been first played at a convention of the (American) National Puzzlers League, Tonto is said to be the invention of Pat McCormick and works as follows:

One player stands up and tries to respond as quickly as possible to questions set by the players, the answers being names of prominent people or historical characters. As soon as he fails, the questioner who caught him out becomes Tonto in his place.

The sort of questions required are:

Is Austrian composer ready to take his medicine like a man? (No – Josef Haydn)
Does Italian portrait subject own her house? (No – Mona Lisa)

Not having played this game in what might be called competitive conditions, I suspect that it is much harder to answer the questions than to think of them in the first place. Here's one I've just thought of:

Is your fireplace called Arthur? (No – Alfred the Great)

Tom Swifties

Any number of players
Mainly for adults
Fun rather than competitive

A punning game well worth reviving is the following, which was the subject of a craze some fifteen years ago and was set as a competition by one of the dailies. (Indeed, I won a fiver for the first of the examples quoted.)

The title derives in a roundabout way from an American

comic character, Tom Swift and his electric aeroplane, popular during the 1920s. The author opened each episode with a sentence such as 'It wasn't my fault,' Tom said, swiftly.

The idea is to find and use an adverb which sums up and puns on a preceding statement or action. Such jokes have flourished in the US for many years. Prize-winning example coming up:

'I've lost my buttonhole,' he said, lackadaisically.

When you've thought about that one, here are a few more to get you in the mood:

'I've eaten your brother William,' said the cannibal, wilfully.
'Tweet, tweet,' said the chicken, cheaply.
'I'm just scraping my ballpoint on the cheese-grater,' he said, pensively.
'I've just finished scraping my ballpoint on the cheese-grater,' he said, expensively.

Turn it into a game in the usual way by going in rotation, and either score points for coming up with new ones or pay forfeits for failing to do so.

Defective Detective

Any number of players
Any age
Fun rather than competitive

This is a rhyming game rather than strictly punning, though the effect is much the same. One player gives a clue to the rhyming title of an Erle Stanley Gardner type of novel, and whoever guesses it first scores a point and sets another one. For example, the clue 'incompetent investigator' produces a book called *The Case of the Defective Detective*. Similarly, 'shy representative' yields *The Case of the Delicate Delegate*, and 'Belgian wart' leads to *The Case of the Flemish Blemish*.

2 · *Performances*

When you tell jokes, does your audience hang on your every word with bated breath until you deliver a punch-line that knocks them out for the count? Or do they shuffle their feet and look at their watches every time you pause to wonder whether you've left an important bit out?

When you rise shakily to your feet and say: 'Unaccustomed as I am to public speaking,' do your listeners find the observation somewhat redundant?

When you hail a bus, does it stop?

In short, are you a good performer? You never know until you've tried, and the party-ish games gathered together in this section (complete with funny hats and false noses) will give you plenty of opportunity to find out. Even if the answer is a mumbled apology rather than a resounding NO, you may well find the practice you gain from these harmless exercises serving you in good stead next time you are invited to launch a battleship or read the saucy telegrams.

The following games vary in the sort of demands they make on you, but the one thing they have in common is the need for fluency. Not everyone may wish to take part (shame!), but those who don't are sure to enjoy the spectacle of others making fools of themselves.

Teapot

Any number of players
Mainly for children
Fun rather than competitive

The principal object of this 'amusant' – to coin a word which ought to exist, even if it doesn't – is to make people laugh. Or to avoid being made to laugh, depending on which way you look at it.

One player is bundled out of earshot while the others agree on a verb. Suppose the verb chosen is 'to sing'. The victim now returns. His task is to discover the hidden verb or to make somebody laugh, whichever is the sooner. This he does by posing questions in which the unknown verb is replaced by the word *teapot*, and to which the respective respondents must reply as if the concealed verb had been used in its place. In this instance, the inquisition might proceed along these lines:

Arnold Where do you usually teapot?
Byron In the bath.
Arnold Does Byron teapot well?
Coleridge No; he usually shatters the windows.
Arnold What would you do if I teapotted all over you?
Dickens Probably stuff cotton-wool in my ears.

As players tire of the game they drop out one by one. When only two remain, they are the winners.

Bananas

Any number of players
Mainly for children
Fun rather than competitive

Bananas will immediately be recognized as a variant of Teapot, except that in this case everyone knows the word involved and the object is merely to avoid laughing.

The first player is chosen by lot (or, if he isn't playing, by Lot's wife) and proceeds to put questions to the others in turn. Whatever the question, it must be answered with the word *bananas*. Whoever laughs before, while or immediately after giving the correct response loses a life (or something) and becomes the next questioner.

The questioner's object is to frame questions to which the bananoid response is most likely to achieve its desired effect: for example, What do you wash your face in each morning?

What do you wear when you go to bed? What's that up your jumper?

As a variant, the questioner may nominate a different word or phrase as the response. *Bananas* tends to lose its flavour after a while.

Hobby Horse

Any number of players
Any age
Fun rather than competitive

From a book of classroom games comes a rapid-response activity which I suspect may amuse many an adult in the right circumstances. It can be done off the cuff if the questioner is good at inventing names, or even, I suppose, knows a lot of people by name; alternatively, write them on slips in advance and either read them out or display them.

To each player in turn the questioner uses the next name on the list in the following formula: 'What's your hobby, Margaret Cholmondley?' To which the player representing Margaret Cholmondley must reply, quick as a flash, 'Mincing cheese-cake' or 'Mangling chemises' or 'Murdering children' or any other activity beginning with the same letters (or sounds) as the stated name.

Anyone who fails to come up with a correct response immediately drops out of play, pays a forfeit or loses a point. You might score a point for an accurate immediate response, doubled if enough people laugh at it.

Quick Thinking

Any number of players
Any age
Fun rather than competitive

Here's another rapid-response exercise taken from a teaching manual. The object, however, is to be ingenious rather than rapid.

Unless you are a quick thinker, you will need to prepare in advance some slips of paper on which are written unlikely objects – the funnier, the better.

As the questioner, you address each player in turn and confront her or him with two objects taken at random from the list, or rather two slips of paper from the hat, and a not necessarily appropriate question. That player must then provide an answer to the question which contains the two items indicated.

For instance:

Items: Bicycle, Doughnut
Q: Why did the chicken cross the road?
A: Because she was out riding her *bicycle* when she saw a bakery on the other side of the road and suddenly fancied a *doughnut*.

Items: Hammer, Spaghetti
Q: What are your immediate plans for the future?
A: When I've finished eating this *spaghetti* I'm going to *hammer* you into the ground.

I suppose the winner is the player whose response evokes the greatest laughter, if any.

Inquisition

Any number of players
Probably better for adults
Fun, but can get nasty

I can't see this game going on all night, but it has been known to while away a minute or two. Basically it is a contest between two players, but it can easily be organized on a tournament basis to produce a single winner at the end.

The first player starts by asking the second a question. The second must reply with a question that follows on plausibly from the first (in the opinion of the other players), to which the first replies with another question, and so on until one of them is fool enough to give a straight answer or bops the other one on the jaw.

The general effect might be as follows:

Arnold What are you doing here?
Byron What's it to you?
Arnold Aren't I allowed to ask?
Byron Why shouldn't you be?
Arnold Then why don't you answer?
Byron What sort of answer do you expect?
Arnold You think I'm expecting?
Byron Er . . . er . . . (oh, balderdash!)

and Arnold has won that round. I suppose winners could score a point for every question that had been asked in the series, but that requires someone to keep count.

Adverbs

Any number of players
Any age
Fun rather than competitive

Do I detect the hand of G. Brandreth in this elegant little parlour game? Very likely, seeing as I pinched it from one of his books.

At each turn one player goes out of the room (or, in my case, switches off his hearing-aid) while the others agree on an adverb for him to discover. Returned to circulation, the victim has three opportunities to put questions to (different) players, each of whom must reply to the best of his or her ability in the manner of the adverb concerned.

After each question, the victim may guess at the adverb. There is no penalty for failure, but a correct guess after the first question earns 3 points, after the second 2, after the third 1 point.

No rule governs the nature of the question that may be put, be it general or specific, personal or impersonal, serious or facetious; nor does it matter whether the answer is true, false or meaningless. All that counts is that it be *delivered* elegantly, brutishly, effeminately, grandiloquently, balbutiently, enthusiastically, languidly, carefully, inquiringly, appealingly, non-committally, laughingly, peremptorily, exploratorily or in whatsoever manner may have been agreed on in the victim's absence. The fun of the game resides in the frequent contrasts between the matter of the replies and the manner in which they are delivered.

> *Fitzgerald* What do you think of my latest translation of the *Ruba'iyat*?
> *Gaskell (enthusiastically)* Extraordinarily boring.

You may possibly find the game improved by awarding a point to the player whose performance leads directly to a correct guess, otherwise there is no point to the performers in giving the game away. If it comes to that, why not start with 5 instead of 3 and award the same score to both the guesser and the performer?

The Railway Carriage Game

Any number of players
Adults and precocious children
Fun but quite competitive

This one sounds eminently Victorian, though I don't find it listed (at least under the present name) in Cassell's *Indoor Amusements and Fireside Fun*.

Two volunteers are selected, under threat of blackmail, and each is secretly given a more or less plausible sentence. They are then seated in such a way as to approximate a railway carriage situation – as the sociologists would say – and required to embark upon conversation. The conversation must as far as possible proceed along plausible lines, and the winner is the first player to produce the sentence he was set as a reasonable continuation of the discussion. One loses if, in the opinion of the company, one forces one's sentence into the conversation without adequate preparation.

Some constraints and provisos are needed to make the game workable. The conversation should start with an introduction or some neutral topic of conversation like the weather, or even with a third 'given' nonsensical sentence, in order to prevent the first conversationalist from gaining an unfair advantage. Then, in accordance with the normal rules of polite conversation in a Victorian railway carriage, players should not be allowed excessive licence in interrupting each other's speeches, whether to deflect them from the subject or to seize upon some word of the other's that may be useful as a springboard to their own sentence. Finally, it is not desirable to insist that the winning sentence should be produced word for word, so long as the key words and their general drift are.

By way of example, let us call our players Byron and Dickens and set them, respectively, the following sentences: 'They say tennis is good for the elbows' and 'I've never eaten whelks with a spoon'. The conversation might run like this, if the by-standers allowed it:

Dickens Looks like rain again.

Byron Yes; pity – I was rather looking forward to a game this afternoon.

Dickens (spotting a possible theme and trying to escape it) Well, you can't play anything with puddles around. Except at the seaside, of course.

Byron Seaside golf course? I prefer tennis myself . . .

Dickens (appealing to the company) Look, I'm not playing if he's going to deliberately mis-hear – (*Cries of 'Shut up!' 'Get on with it!', 'It's only a game!', etc.*) Well, anyway, what I like about seaside puddles is the interesting variety of shellfish you find in them. Do you like shellfish?

Byron No, actually, I prefer tennis, myself, because . . .

Dickens Well I prefer eating. I reckon I've had more hot dinners than you've had games of tennis. I'm particularly fond of whelks . . .

Byron Whelks aren't hot dinners; and what's more, they're very bad for the elbows.
Dickens But they haven't got elbows.
Byron Ah, but if they had, they would undoubtedly play tennis, because they say tennis is very good for the elbows.

This cuts short Dickens's next remark, which was going to be 'Have you ever played tennis with a spoon?' or possibly 'What's your name? Mine's Witherspoon.'

Here are a few target sentences to keep the party boiling.

My aunt tried it once but fell off in the middle.
I once had the same experience with a coconut.
You know, you really ought to get yourself a motorbike.
As the art mistress said to the gardener.
Was that supposed to be your sentence?

A word of advice: the player who answers his opponent's question is usually in danger of being drawn into a conversation trap. Always try to pose questions rather than answer them – though if you have to answer a question with another question, make sure it flows well enough to carry the audience with you; otherwise you may be voted the loser.

Just a Minute

Any number of players
Adults and precocious children
Fun, but daunting

I suppose the reason why even bad radio comedy has always tended to be better than any television comedy is because it is an essentially verbal and therefore witty medium. If, as I believe, the best formulaic radio comedy died with the passing of the brilliant and lovable Kenneth Horne, it has to some extent been compensated for by the development of panel games of the calibre of 'I'm Sorry I Haven't a Clue' and the long-running classic 'Just a Minute'. (And compare the latter with television's 'Call My Bluff' to prove my earlier point.)

Though based on an old parlour game of wide popularity – in my own schooldays it featured prominently as part of an annual 'literary' competition – 'Just a Minute' has been tightened up for radio purposes into a well-organized game format through the genius of Ian Messiter.

The original idea was simply that each player in turn should be given a topic and required to speak as fluently as possible on it for a whole minute without showing signs of mental blockage or nervous breakdown. Messiter's radio format has four performers in competition against one another for points awarded by an umpire in accordance with the following rules:

Each player in turn embarks upon a given subject and tries to keep going for a minute without losing it to someone else. Whoever is speaking when the officially recorded minute is up gains a point, plus an additional point if it was they who started the subject and never lost it.

Timing is stopped at any stage in the proceedings when an opponent challenges the current speaker. If the challenge is upheld, the challenger gains a point and continues the subject for as long as remains of the official minute. If not, the speaker gains a point and continues. *Ex gratia* points are also awarded for clever or witty challenges, even if not upheld.

Challenges can be made – and proved, if necessary – on any of three grounds:

Hesitation, as when the performer pauses unduly, speaks unnecessarily slowly or stumbles over words;

Deviation, when he or she strays from the main subject (or, to stretch a point, deviates from good English or general propriety);

Repetition, which sounds straightforward but, in the event, gives rise to much argument which I consider unsatisfactorily resolved. To my mind, this rule should be exerted to prevent players from saying essentially the same thing over again whether in the same or different words. In practice it is used against repetition by the same speaker of almost any word he may have said in talking about the same topic, other than words included in the subject and grammatical words like articles and prepositions. I think this rule should be interpreted by the spirit rather than by the letter.

Be that as it may, you now have all the ingredients necessary for a good flow of amusement and argument from the company assembled.

Whoever plans the game in advance must act as umpire and, ideally, prepare beforehand enough topics to keep the assembly going for a good hour. About twenty should be ample, allowing for challenges, interruptions and arguments.

Further entertainment value can be added by surreptitiously taping the whole proceedings and playing them back again afterwards.

Some players may require de-hibiting before Just a Minute is announced.

In selecting topics for the minute treatment, bear in mind that speakers are allowed to follow their own interpretation of any ambiguous words they may contain. For example, if the subject were simply given as 'Bats', players could variously talk about cricket bats, vampire bats, 'bats' as a synonym for 'crazy', or even, at a pinch, shares in the British American Tobacco Company. And they may flit from one to the other as often as they wish. Or have to, through failure of inspiration on a previous tack.

Subjects need not be one-worded or even very precise. The following should all be workable amongst imaginative players:

The lesser spotted reed-warbler
Getting lost
Why my hair always looks like this
What the butler really saw
The nineteenth law of thermodynamics
Cleopatra's Needle
How to address royalty
The effects of inflation on bathing suits

Ad Lib, or He Who Hesitates

Any number of players
Adults and older children
Fun rather than competitive

In case Just a Minute is found too fiercely competitive, or too ridiculously anarchic, Ad Lib may be called upon to fill the same sort of gap in a less nerve-racking way. It may also be found more suitable for children.

As before, there is an umpire, who sets the subject and keeps the time. The first player starts talking about the subject and has to keep going for thirty seconds. Interruptions are not allowed. At the end of that time the next must take over the monologue for thirty seconds, and so on for as many players as may be taking part. Neither any one player nor the company as a whole is obliged to stick to the opening subject, so long as each one keeps talking without hesitation after adequately continuing the drift of the previous speaker.

The chief amusement of this game is the discrepancy usually found between the opening subject and the one ended by the last speaker. An element of competition may be introduced by having players drop out if and when they appreciably hesitate, the subject being taken over (and a new half-minute started) from that point. The winner is the last player left talking after all the others have hesitated – and lost.

Yessir, Nossir

Any number of players
Any age
Fun, but nerve-racking

There used to be a radio quiz – subsequently transferred to television, and now, I think, defunct – in which contestants were asked a series of quick-fire questions for a space of half a minute and won a prize if they successfully avoided saying either Yes or No by the time the gong sounded. Strangely, it seemed to play on the nerves of the audience at least as much as on those of the contestant, who would be gonged out as soon as either of the fateful words passed their lips.

The success of the game depended largely, I think, on the cleverness of the questioner, who kept up a barrage of perfectly sequential questions without seeming to strain the subject or repeat himself. It isn't easy to be the victim in a contest that sounds like this, only faster:

Q: Your name is Wright?
A: Right.
Q: Not wrong?
A: Er-er-correct.
Q: And you come from –?
A: From Edgware I come from, I do.
Q: Not Stanmore?
A: N-n-not quite, just near it.
Q: The 25 bus goes there, doesn't it?
A: I don't think so.
Q: Are you certain?
A: Positive.
Q: You didn't say 'Yes', did you?
A: No –
   BONG!

You can play the game this way if you have a questioner who is good at the job. Or you may play the following version of the game, which I should mention that I found in one of Mr Brandreth's books (in case he invented it) under the title Yes No.

Each player is given a number of matchsticks, say five, and all circulate to engage in conversation as the fancy takes them. Anyone who gets another player to say Yes or No gives them a matchstick for it. The first to get rid of all their matchsticks is the winner.

This need not be played with the formal trappings of a game: guests can be given matchsticks and a run-down of the rules when they arrive and keep playing while indulging in whatever people do when they go to parties.

Taboo

Any number of players
Adults and older children
Fun rather than competitive

Similar to the above, and from the same source, is Taboo. I may have changed it somewhat, but the idea is the same.

Each player in turn becomes the questioner or umpire and secretly writes on a slip of paper a word which he chooses as taboo for his round. (Alternatively, prepare slips with taboo words beforehand and get each new questioner to draw one, sight unseen.) He then addresses each other player in turn with a question, which must be adequately answered. His turn as questioner ends as soon as one respondent uses the taboo word in his answer, and he scores as many minus points as questions he put before succeeding. A limit may be set on the number of questions that may be asked. The player with the lowest score is the winner.

Given as taboo the word *help*, suitable questions might include:

What does SOS mean to you?
Why do you blink like that? (Hoping for 'I can't help it')
Does your agèd mother do her own housework?

If the questions are too obvious, it will soon become apparent what word you are seeking, so go carefully.

Spelling Bee

Any number of players
Mainly for children and bad spellers
Competitive rather than fun

I suppose this rather didactic old game fits better into the Performance category than any other.

A bee, in case you have ever wondered, is 'a gathering of persons to unite their labour for the benefit of one individual

or family, or for some joint amusement, exercise or competition (from the bee's habit of combined labour)'. In olden
times, so I've heard tell, society arranged all sorts of jolly bees.
The only one that seems to have come down to us since the
advent of television, at least on my side of the Atlantic, is the
so-called Spelling Bee.

Much as I dislike team games, I feel that the only way of
getting this rather didactic exercise to work is to divide the
company into two teams so that each player is responsible for
thinking of words to be spelt in addition to having to spell some
himself. Some sort of overseer or umpire (or Queen Bee) is
needed to act as dictionary consultant and arbitrator.

One way of organizing the proceedings is as follows:

Each member of a 'batting' team in turn comes to the front,
and has to defend himself against (by correctly spelling) one
word thrown at him by each member of the bowling team. A
point or 'run' is scored for each correct answer; two for a
correct answer challenged by the bowler. When the batsman
has answered one from each bowler he returns to his team.
The teams then change sides: a member of the previously
bowling team now comes out to bat. This continues until each
player has had an innings, when the game ends and the side
with the higher score wins.

More interesting scores are produced if a player who fails to
correctly spell a bowled word is deemed 'out' and ends his
turn.

Spelling Round

Any number of players
Mainly for children
Not very funny or competitive

A non-team spelling game more suitable for children may be
played as follows: the questioner poses a word to be spelt –
let's say *question* – and points to one of the players. Starting
with that player, the word must be spelt around the circle of

players one letter at a time; i.e., the first player says *Q*, the second *U*, the third *E*, and so on. Anyone who makes a mistake or hesitates too long drops out or loses a point.

3 · Proverbials

Proverbs are sayings that supposedly encapsulate the collective wisdom of the ages. *Don't put all your eggs into one basket* sounds quite sensible, meaning much the same as the stockbroker's advice to 'spread your investments', while *Might as well be hanged for a sheep as a lamb* still serves as a good excuse for committing a greater rather than a lesser wrong.

The wisdom of our ancestors, however, might also be seen as a remarkable knack for having it both ways. Only theoretically are proverbs employed to give advice on a course of action before the event. More often, they are dished up as an accompaniment to that good old song 'I Told You So'. That's why proverbs have been noticed to go in contradictory pairs. Whether to say *Look before you leap* rather than *He who hesitates is lost* depends very much on which foregone outcome you are seeking to illustrate. Reference to the collective wisdom of the ages always puts me in mind of Einstein's observation that 'common sense' denotes that burden of prejudices which most people have accumulated by about the age of fourteen. Proverbs, in short, are substitutes for thought, as indeed is demonstrated by the survival of so many in misunderstood or misused forms. 'The exception that proves the rule' has lost its bite since *prove* has come to imply 'afford confirmation of' rather than 'cast doubt on'. Completely pointless nowadays is the phrase 'You can't have your cake and eat it.' Quite demonstrably, this is exactly what you *can* do; what you *can't* do is 'eat your cake and have it'.

Proverbs do, however, offer good playing material to wordgamers, as the following long-popular parlour games illustrate. They all represent a special type of deductive game, in which the object of one team or player is to discover a proverb decided on by the others in accordance with certain conventions of information retrieval. Of course, in so far as proverbs act as commonly known word sequences they can be replaced by other sequences of similar length and nature. Titles of books, plays and films provide one source of material (though I would not recommend re-enactments of one-word titles like *Psycho!*), while another might be current catch-phrases or advertising slogans.

Proverbs

Any number of players
Adults and older children
Fun rather than competitive

One player is sent upstairs to mend the hole in the roof while the others agree on a proverb or popular saying. Let's say it is 'Many hands make light work.' The roof-repairer is then allowed down and has to discover the selected saying, being told only the number of words it contains.

This he does by putting a question to each player in turn (or at random, so long as they all get a chance to participate). The answers must be plausible rather than true, but the essential point is that the answer to the first question must contain, concealed, the first word of the saying; the answer to the second must contain the second word; and so on.

Questions and answers for the example quoted above might sound as follows:

Arnold What can you tell me about Napoleon?
Byron *Many* people say he was too arrogant for his own good.
Arnold Why did you send me upstairs to mend the hole in the roof?
Coleridge Some of us thought it would be a change to see you get your *hands* dirty.
Arnold Who won the Derby in 1922?

Dickens I'm afraid you'll find it rather late if you want to *make* your fortune on it.

Arnold What's a nice girl like you doing in a place like this?

Eliot Well, every woman needs a little *light* entertainment from time to time, between novels.

Arnold Why did the chicken cross the road?

Fitzgerald That's the way it had to go in order to get to *work*.

Arnold Your hidden proverb is: 'People thought fortune needs order.' Or, possibly, 'Many hands make light work.'

One object of the players setting the hidden proverb must be to avoid anything which contains unmistakable key-words. 'He who hesitates is lost' will almost certainly be guessed from the answer to the third question. When you run out of proverbs, start on advertising slogans, or book, film or play titles. To introduce a competitive element, each player scores 1 point per word left upon correctly guessing the phrase – e.g., if Arnold guessed after 'Many' and 'hands', he would score 3 points for 'make light work'.

Shouting Proverbs

Any number of players
Mainly for children
Fun rather than competitive

Let's be honest. Some of the games in this book I have not actually played. But they usually lie in close relation to games that I have played, and I can therefore safely vouch for them. Shouting Proverbs is not one such game, as I can hardly imagine anyone failing to discover the hidden proverb. Nevertheless, it has been so often reported as to occupy the status of a traditional game, if not a classic, and I would be failing in my duty if I did not perpetuate the tradition.

Briefly, then, one player is sent to Coventry while the others agree on a proverb – or cliché, or long-winded book title, or something of the sort. One word of the proverb is assigned to each player. The outcast is then returned to the bosom of his family and seeks to discover the proverb. To this end, at a given signal, the members of the company simultaneously shout out the words individually assigned to them.

It is not clear from existing descriptions whether they all shout the word once only, in complete unison (like the eminently parodiable 'Slain!' in Walton's oratorio *Belshazzar's Feast*), or whether they keep on shouting in an effort to outdo one another in the performance of their individual words. Either way, I cannot imagine that the victim would fail to spot such giveaway words as 'hesitates' (he who being lost) or 'basket' (never put all your eggs into one).

If it does prove too easy, I suggest that the words be shouted once only to start with. If the victim guesses correctly, he scores 3 points; if not, it is shouted a second time for a possible score of 2 points; and then once more, if need be, for a possible 1 point.

Dumb Crambo

Any number of players
Any age
Fun rather than competitive

Dumb Crambo – not to be confused with Cram Dumbo, the elephant-stuffing game – is the original name of a game which is nowadays known as Charades. In this book I reinstate their former titles, since Dumb Crambo is by definition a miming game whereas Charades, properly, calls for verbal play-acting.

You will be fascinated to discover, from a browse through the appropriate entry in the *Oxford English Dictionary*, that Crambo derives from the Latin for bubble-and-squeak. The Latin phrase *crambe repetita* means literally 'cabbage served up again'. Amongst English scholars it developed the metaphorical meaning of 'distasteful repetition', being applied in

this capacity to such things as prayers repeated in parrot
fashion. Hence it became a natural term for a series of
repetitions, not of the same word, but of words that rhyme
with it. Thus in 1706 we find it described as 'A term used
among schoolboys, when in rhiming, he is to forfeit, who
repeats a word that was said before'. It was also known to
Samuel Pepys, from whose entry for 20 May 1660 comes the
confession: 'From thence to the Hague again, playing at
Crambo in the waggon.'

For the original form of Crambo and Charades see page 59
and below. As played today under the, strictly speaking in-
accurate, name of Charades, Dumb Crambo has undergone
some slight modifications.

Usually the object is for one player or team to discover a
phrase or a book, film or play title selected by the others.
Instead of giving the clue of a rhyme, the performers indicate
silently, by means of digital display, first the number of words
in the title, then the number of the word about to be
performed, then the number of syllables contained in that
word and finally the number of the syllable about to be
performed.

Suppose the selected title were *Gone with the Wind*. The
performer (or first performer, if several players are involved)
displays four fingers for the number of words, then one finger
to announce the first of them. He mimes (let us say) waving
good-bye and exiting through a door, representing 'Gone'.

The next performer displays two, then three, then four
fingers, indicating that his mime will reveal the rest of the
phrase. A blustery performance of blowing should suffice for
this.

Had the title been *A Tale of Two Cities*, the last performer
would have displayed five fingers for the fifth word, then two to
show it was composed of two syllables, then one to indicate
that he was about to mime the first. 'Cities' would be represented by 'sit' and then by 'teas' (or possibly golfing tees).

If the game is to be played competitively, it is pointless for
one side or team to guess a subject from the performance of

another, as either the performing team will make it deliberately difficult, even impossible, or, if credit is given for performance, the guessing team will deliberately fail to produce the obvious answer. This is overcome by appointing one person in turn from each team to mime a given title and by allowing both teams to guess. Each wrong guess scores a minus point to the team from which it comes, while a correct guess scores 5 or so to the team that makes it.

Charades

Any number of players
Adults and older children
Fun but hard work

The oldest and perhaps most archetypal parlour game is surely that most magnificent of Victorian amusements, the charade. Here's how it is introduced in the 1881 edition of *Cassell's Book of In-Door Amusements, Card Games and Fireside Fun*:

Although the acting of charades is by no means an amusement of very recent invention, it is one which may always be made so thoroughly attractive, according to the amount of originality displayed, that most young people, during an evening's entertainment, hail with glee the announcement that a charade is about to be acted. It is not necessary that anything great should be attempted in the way of dressing, scenery or similar preparations, such as are almost indispensable to the performance of private theatricals. Nothing is needed beyond a few old clothes, shawls and hats, and a good few actors, or rather, a few clever, bright, intelligent young people, all willing to employ their best energies in contributing to the amusement of their friends. What ability they may possess as actors will soon become evident by the success or failure of the charade.

The word charade derives its name from the Italian word *schiarare* – to unravel or clear up. Suitable as the word may be in some instances, we cannot help thinking that in the majority of cases the acting of a charade has the effect of making the word chosen anything but clear; indeed, the object of the players generally is to make it as ambiguous as possible. As all players of round games know how charades are got up, it would be superfluous to give any elaborate instructions regarding them, though perhaps the following illustration may be useful.

[There follows what appears to be a three-act melodrama, in small print, which opens with] The curtain drawn aside: Miss Jenkyns is seen reclining on her drawing-room couch with a weary look on her face and a book in her hand.

The illustration goes on to disguise the target word Go-Bang (a five-in-a-row game played on a Go board, popular in Victorian England), but, as it is rather long-winded, I had better leave Cassell at this point and invent one of my own.

In the full-blown version of the game the company is divided into two teams, one of which leaves the room *en masse* to prepare their charade, leaving the other to do likewise. Having decided upon a word of two or more syllables and worked out their general line of approach, they return and start their performance.

A spokesman for the performing team announces how many syllables are in the word to be deduced and introduces the first sketch. Let's assume the word is of two syllables. The first sketch is performed in such a way as to incorporate the first half of the word as naturally as possible. For the word I have in mind at the moment the sketch might depict a child being told off for letting its nice plate of beef-fat, lumpy potatoes and cabbage-stumps go to waste. (You know – the sort of dinner which makes English cuisine the worst in the world.)

The second might feature a couple of interior decorators deciding that the woodwork could do with another coat of paint.

If I now suggest that the third and last, in which the whole word has to appear, might depict an audience trying to guess where a conjuror had taken a duplicate card from – 'Up your sleeve', 'Your waistcoat pocket', 'Your gloves', etc. – you will immediately spot the hidden word *waistcoat*, using the word *waste* in the first sketch and *coat* in the second. In real life, however, if anyone still plays such an elaborate game, the two halves of the word and its final whole would have been more carefully embedded in a mass of deliberately confusing verbiage.

To complete the game, the winning team is that which takes the shorter time to deduce its opponents' word. The players may, of course, be formed into more than two teams.

4 · *Alphabeticals*

'This young lady loves you with an H', the King said,
introducing Alice in the hope of turning off the Messenger's
attention from himself.

Through the Looking Glass

The juvenile party games in this section amount to a few
variations on a basic theme, that of thinking up related words
beginning with successive letters of the alphabet. They are of
two sorts: those which are a test of memory, in that each player
must recite the whole list of words that precede his addition to
it, and those which call for quick thinking in the provision of
new ones to add to the list.

Games of this type appear to be very old. The 1881 book of
Indoor Amusements and Fireside Fun credits to Samuel Foote,
the eighteenth-century comic actor, an anecdote concerning
the ladies Cheere (presumably Helen Cheere, c. 1710–60),
Fielding and Hill. They were amusing themselves by playing
the children's game of I Love My Love. Lady Cheere began by
saying, 'I love my love with an N, because he is a (k)Night.'
Lady Fielding followed with, 'I love my love with a G, because
he is a Giustus' (of the Peace?). Lady Hill added, 'I love my
love with an F, because he is a Fizician.'

'So much', comments the Victorian editor, 'for the spelling
powers of the ladies in the olden times' – it evidently not
occurring to him for one moment that they might have been
joking.

A few games of this sort are described here to give you the
flavour of the thing. As the old song goes, if you want any
more you must sing it yourself.

I Love My Love

Any number of players
Mainly for children
Fun rather than competitive

'I love my love with an A', announces Arnold, 'because she is Attractive. I hate her with an A because she is Arrogant. I took her to Alperton and treated her to Apples and Apricots. Her name is Angela and she comes from Angola.'

'I love my love with a B', begins Byron, 'because she is Bounteous. I hate her because she is Belligerent. I took her to Balham and gave her Bluebells and Belladonna. Her name is Bertha and she comes from Bangkok'.

I'd better not do any more, or there will be nothing left for your imagination. Each player in turn does the next letter of the alphabet. In this and all following games it is reasonable to allow the words for X to begin with EX- if desired.

To prevent too much thinking ahead, I suggest that, instead of playing in strict rotation, each player points to anyone of his choice to follow after him.

A competitive element may be introduced by losing points for faltering or by making defaulting players drop out until only one remains.

The *memory version* of the game goes as follows:

'I love my love with an A because she is Adorable.'
'I love my love with a B because she is Adorable and Beautiful.'
'I love my love with a C because she is Adorable and Beautiful and Cuddly.'*

And so on: each player recites the list to date and adds a new one. Adverbs may be added, thus: 'Because she is Absolutely Adorable, Beautifully Bouncy, Capriciously Charming . . .' Or

---

* Incredibly, while the verb *cuddle* is known to the compilers of *Chambers Twentieth Century Dictionary*, the adjective *cuddly* is not. They must have suffered from deprived childhoods and unhappy love lives.

verbs and adverbs: 'Because she Dances Delightfully, Excites Enigmatically, Flirts Facetiously . . .'

My examples are all feminine for obvious reasons. Players are expected to switch pronouns according to personal tastes.

The Travelling Alphabet

Any number of players
Mainly for children
Fun rather than competitive

'I am going on a journey to Amsterdam,' says the first player.
   'What will you do there?' demand all and sundry.
   'I shall Answer Amazing Advertisements,' says the first.
   The second, having declared himself bound for Belize or Bakersfield or wherever, and having been asked his intentions, continues: 'I shall Boil Brilliant Beans,' or something else expressive of the letter B.
   This continues until the twenty-sixth player (or the fifth, if only seven are playing) has been to Zimbabwe for the purpose of Zincking Zoological Zithers, when it will be time to play something else.

The A-to-Z Banquet

Any number of players
Mainly for children
Fun rather than competitive

A memory game for people with strong stomachs.

   'I went to a banquet and ate some Anchovies,' says the first.
   'I went to a banquet,' continues the second, 'and ate Anchovies and Broccoli.'
   The third will have eaten Anchovies, Broccoli and Cheese, to which the fourth might add Dates and the fifth Eggplant. And so on.
   Very sensitive players may find this game more difficult to get through than it appears.

Hypochondriac

Any number of players
Mainly for (older) children
Fun rather than competitive

'I went to hospital because I had Appendicitis.'
 'I went to hospital because I had Appendicitis and Boils.'
 'I had Appendicitis, Boils and Cholera.'
 The winner is the first player to pass out.

I Packed My Bag

Any number of players
Mainly for children
Fun rather than competitive

'I went to Alaska and in my bag I packed an Anorak.'
 'I went to Barbados and in my bag I packed a Boot.'
 'I went to Chile and in my bag I packed a Corset.'
 The memory version of this game is more amusing. 'I went away', says the first, non-committally, 'and in my bag I packed an Alligator.' The second will have packed an Alligator and a Balloon, the third an Alligator, a Balloon and a Corkscrew . . . Need I go on?

Note: All the foregoing games may be complicated, if not improved, by playing in rotation but not necessarily in alphabetical order. Each letter of the alphabet must be used once, however, and anyone who embarks on a letter that has already been exhausted must drop out, lose a point or pay a forfeit.

Oral Alphabent

Any number of players
Adults and older children
Fun but skill-demanding

An alphabent is a sentence or paragraph of twenty-six words beginning with successive letters of the alphabet – such as:

Although Banjos Can Do Exceedingly Fast Gavottes, Harps Invariably Jam. Knowing Lithuanian Musicians Now Openly Prohibit Quadrilles, Rumour Suggesting That Unimpeachable Virgins Willingly Xerox Your Zither.

Alphabents in their more effective written form are further discussed on p. 120. But they can give rise to much amusement as an oral game played in the following way:

Playing in rotation, the first performer opens by announcing a word beginning with A, the second continues with B, the third with C, and so on. Successive words must, of course, follow on grammatically from those immediately preceding so as to gradually build up a sentence. If a natural break is reached before the alphabet is completed, the first word of the new sentence must bear some meaningful relation to what has gone before. Each player scores a point for each word he announces, and the first to fail to do so loses a point. Points may be recorded by raising and lowering fingers during the performance.

It is a good idea to tape the performances, in case brilliant examples are thrown up which might otherwise be forgotten.

5 · *Sequentials*

These are in the nature of party games intended for fun rather than competition, though part of the fun may well consist in imposing forfeits on players who fail to keep the pot boiling. The heading refers to the feature which these games have in common, namely, that each in turn must contribute a word or phrase to the ones that have gone before, in such a way as to bear some previously determined relationship to them – for example, that they should rhyme, or begin with the same letter, or continue the sense (or nonsense, as the case may be).

Buzz, Bizz and Roman Buzz

Any number of players
Any age
Fun and competitive

I used to play this at school under the impression that it was a mathematical game, but have since come across it in a book on word games, so why omit it on that score?

Players arrange themselves in a theoretical circle and play the game by numbering off, *One*, *Two*, etc. Whenever a player's number is a multiple of three, or contains the figure three, he must say *buzz* instead; otherwise he drops out. Play continues until all but one have dropped out or an agreed target (say 100) is reached.

The game may be varied in several obvious ways. One is to change the figure and multiple concerned. Another is to introduce a second, the most popular being seven. If a number contains or is a multiple of three, say *buzz*, as before; if it contains or is a multiple of seven, say *bizz*; if both, say *bizz-buzz* or *buzz-bizz*.

It occurs to me that advanced players may like to number off in Roman numerals, thus: Aye, aye-aye, *buzz*, aye-vee, vee, *buzz*, *bizz*, vee-aye-aye-aye, *buzz*, ex, and so on.

The Tennis-Elbow-Foot Game

Any number of players
Any age
Fun rather than competitive

The players sit in a circle, or square, or pear shape, or indeed any arrangement that enables them to see at a glance whose turn it is next and how long it will be before their own comes round again.

The first player announces a word, which could be *tennis* or any one of pretty well 300,000 others. The next in turn must immediately respond with a word clearly related to the first, such as *ball* or *racquet* or *net* or even *elbow*. The third player might then come up with *foot*, the next with *boot*, and so on.

Anyone who fails to respond immediately with a sensibly connected word, or repeats one that has already been used, or collapses in uncontrollable hysterics, drops out of the game.

The winner is the last player left in, or the first to develop genuine symptoms of tennis elbow (whichever is the sooner).

Free Association

Any number of players
Any age
Fun rather than competitive

In this version of Tennis-Elbow-Foot each succeeding player must come up with the first word that comes to mind as a result of the previous one. It need not be sensibly connected; on the contrary, the whole point of the game is to see what peculiar connections lie within the murky recesses of everybody else's

minds. Even more interesting are the mental blocks that
sometimes arise when one word or concept completely fails to
evoke another in the mind of the next player.

It is difficult to tell who has won this game and why. There
are those who claim it has some form of psychological
therapeutic value, but I don't believe a word of it.

Mornington Crescent

Any number of players
Adults and older children
Fun rather than competitive

For many years now BBC Radio 4 has run something called
'I'm Sorry, I Haven't a Clue', which is described as 'the
antidote to radio panel games'. One of the rounds that
occasionally appears is called Mornington Crescent, the rules
of which are never explained and which I have never been able
to deduce from the way the game is played – probably because
no one is intended to do so anyway. (One player starts with
'Mornington Crescent'. The others in succession come up with
other London place-names, and this continues until someone
repeats 'Mornington Crescent', at which point nobody is
declared a winner and they pass on to something else.)

They also play a variation of Tennis-Elbow-Foot, which may
have a name, but I've either never heard it or else forgotten it.
I have therefore combined the two and present here the second
game under the name of Mornington Crescent, which you
must admit has a certain air about it.

> They made me a present
> Of Mornington Crescent –
> They threw it
> A brick at a time

once sang, as I recall, a certain Gilbert O'Sullivan.

In this game the next player must come up with a word
which not only has not been announced before but also has
absolutely *no* demonstrable connection with the previous

word. If anyone else can show that a given word is related to the previous one then the challenged player is out of the game. Needless to say, a player who does not respond almost immediately is also out.

Mornington Crescent may sound impossibly silly, but in fact it is more demanding than Tennis-Elbow-Foot.

A typical game might begin as follows:

Tennis
Bacon and eggs
Mornington Crescent
Six o'clock
Challenge: 'I get up at six o'clock in the Mornington.'
  (Fourth player drops out.)

Heads and Tails

Any number of players
Adults and older children
Competitive but fun

A category of names or objects is given, let us say Towns. Each player in turn must announce the name of a town which (a) has not been mentioned already and (b) begins with the last letter of the previous town. Such a sequence might begin as follows:

London
Norwich
Hartlepool
Littlehampton

. . . and so on. A player drops out if he fails to answer within a few seconds, or repeats a name, or if the name he quotes does not begin with the required letter.

This makes a good general knowledge quiz for younger players. The game can be spiced up in either of two ways. A particularly nasty one is to eliminate a player whose answer begins and ends with the same letter. Another is to play against a timer that sounds an alarm after a predetermined interval. In this case players do not drop out; instead, when the alarm sounds, the last player to have announced a valid name is the winner, and/or the person whose turn it is to speak is the loser and has to pay some sort of forfeit.

Trailers

Any number of players
Adults and older children
Fun rather than competitive

This is the verbal equivalent of a game which I describe elsewhere as a pencil-and-paper game.

The first player announces a two-word compound; thereafter each in turn must come up with a compound whose first half is the second half of the previous one. A player who cannot think of one may challenge anyone to come up with an answer, and drops out if someone suggests one – otherwise he is the winner and/or the previous player is the loser. For example:

Boathouse
House warming
Warming pan
Pancake
Cakestand

Crambo

Any number of players
Adults and older children
Fun rather than competitive

For the venerable history of rehashed cabbage (which is what Crambo means) see page 45. Here is a slightly updated version of it, also known as Rhyme in Time.

The first player thinks of a rhythmic phrase or short sentence and announces it to the assembled company. Each in turn thereafter must spontaneously come up with a line of similar length and rhythm – but don't be too strict about that – which rhymes with the preceding one(s). A player drops out, or is declared the loser, if he dries up, repeats a previous rhyme or fails to rhyme satisfactorily.

A game might begin as follows:

> Never say die
> Look at the sky
> Who said pigs can't fly?
> Wasn't me. Why?
> Crisps make me cry
> Or so you imply

. . . and so on.

You might also insist that each new phrase bear some obvious, or at least explainable, relationship to the previous one, as do lines 2 to 4 and 5, 6 above; but as this makes the game rather more difficult each player should be allowed a few seconds' thinking time.

An awful responsibility rests with the first player, who must be careful to choose an ending capable of yielding a long enough sequence of rhymes. I suppose you could devise some sort of score for the game along the following lines. A game consists of as many rounds as there are players. A round ends when somebody fails to rhyme in accordance with the rules. The starter keeps count of the number of lines produced by the whole group. (He need only count his own in order to keep adequate track, of course.) When the round ends, the starter scores a point for each line and the loser scores the same number of minus points. If the starter is also the loser he scores only minus points.

Life Sentence

Any number of players
Adults and older children
Fun, but requires concentration

Here is a variation of Heads and Tails which I have just thought of. It looks rather more difficult, but I'm sure there are players who will rise to the challenge.

The object is to produce a plausible sentence or series of connected sentences (running consecutively, as they say), to which each player contributes one word in turn, and such that each new word begins with the last letter of the previous one. A player who is unable to continue plausibly drops out, scores a demerit, pays a forfeit or loses six months' remission, as agreed beforehand.

Such a sentence might run as follows:

> When no one expects sincere explanations, several lies seem most telling . . .

This sentence sounds as if it has reached a natural end, and the next player is stuck for a suitable continuation beginning with G.

Acronymia

Any number of players
Adults and older children
Requires concentration

Initial sentences is the plain title of the following game, which comes from a classroom aid. Despite its originally intended setting, I see it as quite challenging to adults and possibly boring to children, but should be happy to be proved wrong. To some extent it may be regarded as a close relative of Ghosts, and, as such, admits of a challenging rule.

Players arrange themselves in such a way as to be able to play in endless rotation. The first (designated by whatever means you prefer) must start a sentence by announcing, as the subject of it, a name, e.g. John. The sentence is continued by each in turn adding a new word to it – *but* in such a way that the initials of the words of the sentence spell a word. For example, the sentence might continue:

John Expects A Nice Surprise,

the initials of which spell the word JEANS.

If played the 'ghostly' way, the player who completes a word of four or more letters is the loser and scores a demerit or pays a forfeit. Or a player may challenge the previous one to prove that the initial provided by his word will enable a word to be made.

Otherwise, play continues until one player cannot add a word which either continues the sentence or contributes to the acronymic construction of a word. That player is the loser, and/or the one before him the winner.

Up the Dictionary

Not too many players
Mainly for adults
Competitive and requires concentration

This game is credited to Dave Silverman and was first published in *Word Ways* under the title Last Word, which is unfortunately neither distinctive nor distinguished.

An agreed length of word is chosen, let us say five letters. The first player announces such a word beginning with A – for example, ACORN. Thereafter each in turn must announce a word which (a) comes later in the dictionary than the previous one and (b) contains at least one 'crash' with the previous word – that is, at least one common letter in the same position.

Such a game might run as follows:

A C O R N
B L U R T (R in same position as in ACORN)
Y O U T H (U in same position as in BLURT)

Z O N E D
Z O W I E (it's in *Chambers*!) – wins.

If you find the end of the game becoming predictable after a while, try this variant: each new word must contain exactly one crash with the previous word (not more) and must either begin with the same initial (the only crash allowed) or with the next letter of the alphabet. This variant may be shortened by kicking off with a word whose initial is O or P or even further up the dictionary.

6 · *Ghostlies*

The classic game of Ghost is one of several based on a distinctive theme which should appeal to crossword solvers. A ghost is a sequence of letters which do not form a whole word but which can be filled out with other letters to form one. For example, the letters OWH may be regarded as the 'ghost' of the filled out or fully embodied word HOWDAH. Crosswords, you see, are full of ghosts, and much of the pleasure of the solving lies in gradually laying them. Vehicle licence- or number-plates are also haunted, as any word-gaming driver is aware.

Ghost

Not too many players
Adults and older children
Requires concentration

The first player announces the first letter of a word, without bothering to think what the word is – for example T.

The second adds a second letter, which must be one capable of following the first in some real word. After T, for instance, he might say A or any other vowel, or H, R or W. He would not say D, as he would then be challenged to produce a word beginning with TD and would lose.

After A, the third (or first again if only two are playing) might add L, thinking perhaps of TALBOT or TALISMAN or suchlike.

Play continues in this way with a new letter being added to the string at each turn. Each new letter must be capable of producing a word in conjunction with the preceding ones, but the whole point of the game is to avoid being the player who actually completes a word. A player who does complete a word is the loser of the round, and a new one begins. Alternatively (depending on how many are playing) he drops out – becomes a 'ghost' – for the rest of the game, which ends when only two are left in and one of them wins. Or he may 'lose a life' and become a ghost when he has lost three lives, or any other agreed number.

Two- and three-letter words are permitted, by the way; it is not until the fourth is added that a finished word loses the round.

A three-player game might begin as follows:

1. T
2. TA
3. TAL (thinking of TALC, TALL, etc., but not TALBOT or TALISMAN as he would be the one to complete the word)
1. TALO (thinking of TALON)
2. TALOM (bluffing)
3. Challenge!

This game came to an untimely end, as the second player could only think of TALON and would have lost had he said N. As a desperate measure he tried to bluff the next player into thinking there was a word beginning with TALOM. In the unlikely event that the third player had fallen for it, he might have attempted a double bluff by adding another letter, in which case the second player would have challenged it and not lost the round.

Challenges may be made on either of two grounds: that the last letter added forms a word, or that it prevents any valid word from being made. In the first case the onus is on the challenger to prove that such a word exists if no one else has heard of it; in the second, the challengee must announce and (if necessary) prove the existence of a word which can be produced by following on from the letter he has added. Whichever of the two players concerned is in the wrong loses the round or a 'life'.

Superghost

Not too many players
Adults and older children
Requires concentration

As above, but each in turn may add a letter to either end of the existing string. For example:

1. T
2. T A
3. P T A (thinking of CAPTAIN)
1. P T A G
2. Challenge!
1. . . . (see page 227 if you can't think of the answer)

In this version words of up to four letters are not penalized: only from the fifth onwards do players lose by completing a word.

Anaghost

Not too many players
Mainly for adults
Requires concentration

It is hard to imagine this logical extension of Ghosts being played without the aid of pencil and paper, but I dare say some players will be brave (or fanatical) enough to embark upon it.

In this version, as you might expect, letters are not added in any particular position of the word, and anyone may be challenged for adding a letter in such a way as to produce an anagram. A short example:

1. T
2. CT
3. CET
1. CEHT (thinking of CHEST)
2. CEHRT (thinking of THRICE)

3. Challenge: everyone knows that CHERT is a compact flinty chalcedony (etymology dubious)!

Anaghosts does not permit short words. After T, for example, the second player would have lost by announcing A.

Ultraghost

Not too many players
Mainly for adults
Requires concentration

Another case of great minds thinking alike. Having devised and played the following ghostly variant for some time I received from America an account of a broadly similar game played at the 1978 National Puzzlers' League Convention and credited to one 'Ajax', of pseudonymous word-puzzling fame. It certainly follows the same lines as Ultraghost, though not going quite as far.

Ultraghost derives from that unconscious habit of all word-lovers who are also drivers of turning the letters on car number-plates into words. Indeed, Ajax's game is called the Licence Plate Game. As played at the Convention, cards were held up bearing three-letter sequences and the object was to see who could come up with the shortest word incorporating those letters in the stated sequence, though not necessarily consecutively. For instance, PZM yielded PUZZLEMENT quite quickly, which was then beaten by the shorter TRA-PEZIUM; XLP produced EXCULPATE, followed by the considerably better OXLIP.

My game introduces two further constraints, as will be seen, and I should perhaps warn at this point that it is not exactly a party game. It is ideally played with some sort of letter-randomizing device, such as a computer or a set of cards or tiles from a proprietary word game. Failing that, you need at least four players to make the game successful.

It works as follows.

Having thought for a moment or two and declared

themselves ready, the first three players announce three letters of the alphabet in rapid succession (no collusion). This serves as the randomizing device for the fourth player, who is on the spot, so to speak. His object is to come up with the best possible word which *begins* with the first letter quoted, *includes* the second and *ends* with the third.

The required word must be at least four letters in length (so that it doesn't matter if the three given letters happen to form a word) but otherwise must be as short as possible. The player in turn may be given a time limit of one minute, if so agreed beforehand, but in fact the game is designed to make time consumption disadvantageous and I always insist on a minimum ten seconds' thinking time before any answer may be made.

For coming up with a suitable word, the player whose turn it is scores 3 points, unless any opponent *immediately* announces a better one. (Opponents do not have extra thinking time for this.)

A better word is one which fits the pattern and is also shorter (though four is the minimum permitted length). In this case the player scores only 1 point instead of 3. Nothing is scored by the opponent who beats it.

An alternative form of better word is one which is the same length as the one stated by the player whose turn it is, but earlier in the alphabet. For example, if the given letters were P A O and the player in turn said PIANO, an opponent could beat it with PHARO – same length, but earlier in the dictionary. In this case the player in turn scores 2 instead of 3. Of course, another opponent could go better by saying PACO, which is shorter, thus reducing the score to 1 point.

If the player whose turn it is cannot think of a word, he may either give up or challenge. If he gives up, he scores 1 point if nobody else immediately announces a suitable word, but loses 1 point if somebody does have one. The same applies to a challenge, but the value is doubled – 2 points if no one has a word, minus 2 points if someone has.

The game is played up to any agreed target, e.g. 15 points.

Here are twenty-six ultraghosts which you may like to embody rather than look them up on page 227. Remember, in each case you are required to find the shortest word of four or more letters which begins with the first, includes the second and ends with the last.

A U E	N I H
B E Y	O G I
C J Y	P O O
D O G	Q L M
E O W	R T C
F F F	S Y P
G L C	T F H
H E M	U W D
I V Y	V U E
J X E	W O M
K W N	X P E
L N H	Y R M
M T X	Z A T

7 · Deductives

Deductive word games, as the name denotes, are those in which one player or team tries to discover a word or phrase agreed upon by the others. This differs from most of the games in the book, which, by contrast, are 'constructive', in that the object is to compose words from given elements.

The method of discovering hidden words or phrases is naturally based on asking questions designed to elicit helpful clues. The questions have to be more or less oblique, of course – you can't simply ask outright what the hidden word is! Thus the way in which the games differ from one another lies in the type or obliquity of the questions that may be asked and the information which may be given.

There is quite a range in this class of games, to which also belong the rather special case of Proverbials introduced on page 42. Very roughly, I have arranged them from easiest to hardest, or from most to least attractive to children.

I Spy

Any number of players
Not suitable for adults
Fun rather than competitive

The ultimate deductive word game is, of course, I Spy – that exquisite form of intellectual torture for motorists whose families insist on playing it in the car on holiday trips to the opposite end of the country.

In case the game is completely new to you, suffice to say that one player looks around and ritually announces: 'I spy with my little eye something beginning with X' (or whatever may have caught his fancy). The others then try to guess what it is by calling *xylophone*, *xebec*, *xylem*, *xyster*, etc. Eventually they give up and the caller is lucky to escape with his life after revealing the answer to be *exercise-book*.

Players do not call in turn, or any other sort of order, and a correct guesser becomes the next spy. Scoring systems can be invented.

Key Word

At least six players
Any age
Competitive but light-hearted

This game comes from a schoolteacher's book of language games and (or but) can be varied in level to suit any age. It is a team game, which does not fill me with enthusiasm, but has other merits to compensate. One player writes slips containing suitable words in advance and plays the teacher's role as umpire or question-master.

At each round of play two members of each team step forward. One of each pair is designated 'blind' and sits with his back to the questioner. His partner stands in front of him facing the questioner. The questioner holds up a card or slip bearing a word which the 'blind' players have to deduce from clues given them by their partners, both of whom can see it.

The procedure is as follows. The standing partner of the left team gives a one-word clue to the target word, and his blind partner takes a guess at it. If it is wrong, the standing partner of the right team gives a second one-word clue and his blind partner has one guess at it. This continues in alternation until one of the blind players correctly guesses the target word. His team then scores a point – or, if you prefer something more sophisticated, scores 11 points less the number of one-word clues already heard – i.e. a correct guess after the first clue scores 10, and so on. If neither side has got the target word after ten clues have been heard (five from each side) the round ends. In this case it may be agreed that the following round is played for double the score.

At children's level, a target word might be something like *spoon*, evoking such clue words as *eat*, *handle*, *metal*, *useful*, *dessert* and so on. At an advanced level it could be almost anything, so the questioner should indicate to the blind players at least what part of speech they are looking for (common name, proper name, adjective, etc.). It could even be a word with different meanings, leading to mixed clues; for instance, *strike* might be indicated by such words as *match*, *workers*, *hit*, and so on.

Twenty Questions

A small group of players
Any age
Competitive but light-hearted

A BBC radio game of many years' standing, Twenty Questions started out as a Victorian parlour game and may even be much older.

In the original version one player, whom I will call the challenger, writes the name of a common object on a slip of paper. The aim of the other players is to discover what it is. This they do by asking questions about it – either in rotation or at random, as agreed beforehand – to which the only permissible answers are Yes and No. Up to twenty such questions may be asked and answered; if the object has not been discovered by the twentieth question, then the challenger has won. An outright guess ('Is it a toothpick?') counts as a question, as does any question to which the answer is No. Questions answered Yes do not count as part of the twenty, and a Yes answer entitles the questioner to ask another if play is proceeding in strict rotation. The player who guesses the object becomes the new challenger.

In practice it may come as a surprise to discover how much can be learnt about an object from a series of yeas and nays:

Are we looking for one special thing? – No
Is there one in this room? – No
Is there one in the street? – No
In the garden? – Yes
A plant of some sort? – No
Is it alive? – No (*trying not to laugh*)
(What's funny?) Was it alive and is now dead? – No
A bird table? – No
Does it look as if it ought to be alive? – Yes
Not that horrible stone frog thing by the pond? – No
A garden gnome? – Yes.

If the challenger cannot answer Yes or No without doubt he should say nothing (pull a face, perhaps) and discount the question. At the third question above, for instance, the challenger wondered at first whether he should answer No because the gnome was not actually in the street, or Yes because there was at least one in an area which could be described as being 'in the street' as opposed to 'miles away somewhere else'.

The game can be extended in scope to include not only things but also people or places. In this case the challenger should start by announcing whether the object of the inquiry is a person, place or thing.

The radio version of the game goes further still. The object of the inquiry can be pretty well anything you can think of, as abstract or concrete and as real or imaginary as you like. Nothing in the rules would prevent such 'objects' as:

Liquorice allsorts
Pandemonium
The daring young man on the flying trapeze
A black hole
The Black Hole of Calcutta
Boot blacking
Bootlicking behaviour
A rose-red city, half as old as time
The North Pole

In this case the challenger conventionally starts by announcing that the object is animal, vegetable, mineral or abstract. It may be more than one at the same time – for instance, 'a stitch in time' is abstract 'with strong vegetable connections', since stitching might imply cotton and cotton is of vegetable origin. Or it may be one or another depending on which of several possible meanings is considered – for example, 'sloth' could be animal or abstract but not both at once. (Incidentally, anything made of plastic is mineral, since plastic is mostly derived from oil; and a common response to the announcement 'vegetable with mineral connections' is the question 'Are we looking for paper with printing on it?')

As performed on radio the questioners are not obliged to pose Yes/No questions and the challenger is generally expected to answer other questions of any description provided that he does not give too much away. (All questions count, regardless of the answer.) The regular players of the game, however, are so adept at following up leads and framing useful questions that they almost invariably win. If this happens in your games it might be a good idea to go back to the Yes/No format. Even so, where the quizzer has chosen an object with two or more meanings, he should specify which of them he is answering – for example, 'Yes, but not in the mineral sense'. It would anyway, I feel, do no harm to ban objects treated ambiguously.

Any form of the game may be played with a point-scoring system if desired, for which purpose the following is suggested:

The winner is the first player to reach 100 points. Questioners must put their questions in turn rather than at random. The challenger scores 1 point for every question asked before the object is guessed, plus a bonus of 10 if he wins (making 30 points). If the challenger wins he remains the challenger for the next round. A questioner who correctly guesses the object scores 10 points and becomes the next challenger. Guesses (as opposed to questions) may be made out of turn at any time, but a wrong guess made out of turn imposes a penalty of 10 points on the questioner who made it. (There is no penalty if a questioner uses his turn to make a guess instead of pose a question.)

Who Am I?

Any number of players
Any age
Light-hearted but requires thought

Who Am I? may be regarded as a cross between Twenty
Questions and Botticelli, which follows. Children should enjoy
it.

The quizzer thinks of a famous person, or historical or
fictional character, and announces the initial of their principal
name (normally the surname in the case of real people). The
questioners have to find out who the person is by a series of
questions eliciting Yes/No answers. If the subject has not been
guessed after twenty questions the quizzer has won.

Botticelli

A small group of players
Mainly for adults
Competitive but can be fun

This is one of two games my wife and I played on a snow-
bound honeymoon. No doubt we were undergoing some kind
of identity crisis at the time, or indulging in fantasy role-
playing. (The other one was Piquet.) But more players make
for a better game, and as Botticelli is a good excuse for general
knowledge show-offs to show off generally and knowledgeably,
I dare say it will be enjoyed more by adults than by children.

As in Who Am I?, above, the quizzer assumes an identity
and states the initial of the principal name. At this stage he
gives no further information.

The questioners start by putting a series of 'specific questions'
to the quizzer, to which the latter must respond appropriately
in the following way. Suppose he gave the initial C, then:

Q: Are you a silent comedy film star?
A: No, I'm not Charlie Chaplin.
Q: Were you taken for a ride by A. Hitler?

A: No, I'm not Neville Chamberlain.
Q: Were you poisoned by your wife Agrippina?
A: I, Claudius? Never!
Q: Are you the female author of novels emphasizing family relationships?
A: Er – Agatha Christie?

This response being greeted with contempt, Ivy Compton-Burnett has won the questioner the right to a 'general question' requiring a Yes/No answer:

Q: Are you male or female?
A: Yes.
Q: I withdraw the question. Are you male?
A: No.

Two bites are not normally allowed at the cherry, but as the first question was clearly nonsensical, the second has been allowed on this occasion. But don't make the same mistake again.

The questioners now go back to their series of specific questions, to each of which the quizzer, if his identity is not deduced, must reply with the name of a person who could have fitted the question. As soon as he cannot answer again, the questioner may pose another general, Yes/No question, such as 'Are you American?' or 'Legendary?' or 'Generally regarded as evil?'

The same specific question may be asked more than once and require a different answer each time; for example:

Q: Are you an historical Catherine?
A: I'm not Catherine the Great.
Q: Are you another historical Catherine?
A: No, not Catherine of Aragon.
Q: Are you another historical Catherine?
A: Nor Catherine de' Medici.
Q: Are you, by any remote chance, an historical Catherine?
A: No, I'm not Catherine Wheel.

The quizzer has evidently run out of real Catherines – there are still forty per cent of Henry's remaining wives to come – and now has to face a general question.

Theoretically, the round ends when someone has deduced the quizzer's identity, and the successful questioner assumes the next alias. But if it looks as if the round is going on for ever you may agree to end when a certain time is up, or when the quizzer has successfully negatived a given number of questions, say thirty.

Backenforth

Any number of players
Adults and older children
Fun rather than competitive

Nobody seems to have described this game before, though it is easy to think of and fun to play.

One player reads or announces a word backwards. The first person to call it out forwards scores a point. If an incorrect call is made, the caller loses a point and the questioner gains one.

A certain degree of latitude must be allowed in deciding how the back-words should be pronounced. A purely phonetic reverse pronunciation of NIGHT, for example, would be TINE, whereas a literal reversal yields THGIN. I think the game is better if the questioners follow their own inclinations in this respect, but it should certainly be permissible, if not at times compulsory, to keep intact such digraphs as CH, SH and TH where they represent a single sound. For example, THUS reversed should be SUTH, not the unpronounceable SUHT; similarly, the reverse of CHOP is PO(T)CH and of SHOP, POSH. I also keep NG intact: SINGING backwards is quite pro-nounceable as NGINGIS, even though English words do not naturally begin with that sound. No objection should be raised, however, to GNIGNIS, provided that the Gs are sounded.

The questioner only is allowed to write his word down, in order to help him pronounce it effectively. The others must use their minds' eyes and/or ears to solve it.

There are two ways of playing: either each person in turn is the questioner or the successful guesser of a back-word becomes the next questioner.

Clue Words

A small group of players
Adults and older children
Light-hearted but requires concentration

Gyles Brandreth is to be credited with this novel variation on a theme.

One player thinks of a word of eight different letters as the target word and gives up to three clues as to its identity.

The first clue is a word of three (different) letters, each of which occurs in the target word. Each opponent in turn may have one guess at the target word. If successful, that player scores 3 points and sets the next word; if not, there is no penalty and the second clue is given.

The second clue is a word of four (different) letters, and one guess each is made again. Success this time scores 2 points. Failure elicits the third clue, which is a word of five different letters taken from the target, for a score, if successfully guessed, of 1 point.

If the target word is not discovered, the setter scores a point and the next in turn takes over.

Shaffe's Game

Two players
Mainly for adults
Requires concentration

A version of Jotto or Crash, described in the pencil-and-paper section of this book, Shaffe's Game is simplified to make it playable *viva voce* – or in the car, whichever you prefer. I dare say the game has several independent originators. I got it from *Games for the Superintelligent* by James F. Fixx, who in turn got it from a correspondent called Samuel A. Shaffe.

One player thinks of a five-letter word and the other has to find out what it is. (You should try it one at a time at first, postponing simultaneous play until you get used to the exercise.) The guesser does so by announcing other five-letter words, in response to each of which the setter tells him how many letters of the test word are contained in the target word. For instance, if the target word is S K U N K the following test words produce the stated figures:

    QUITE = 1
    BRAND = 1
    GLOOM = 0
    SLYLY = 1
    STICK = 2
    STUCK = 3

and so on. The position of corresponding letters doesn't matter: all that counts is their number. It may be agreed that the target word must contain five different letters, though this need not apply to the test words.

Of course, the game may be played with words of any agreed length.

Aesop's Mission

Any number of players
Adults and Victorian children
Fun, but irritating

Such is the Victorian name of a game that appears in many guises. 'One of the gentlemen well acquainted with the game undertakes to represent Aesop,' says the 1881 *Book of In-Door Amusements . . . and Fireside Fun*, continuing, 'In order to do so more effectually, he may put a cushion or pillow under his coat to imitate a hump, provide himself with a thick stick for a crutch, make a false nose, and put a patch over one eye.'

I must say this sounds to me more like Long John Silver than

Aesop, but it does go to show how thoroughly people entered into games before television came to take their minds off everything. No Victorian parlour, evidently, was complete without its thick stick, hump substitute, eye-patch and bucket of *papier-mâché* for producing the instant false nose.

> *Mamma* Might one propose a game of Aesop's Mission?
> *Papa* A splendid notion! – Emily, pray be so good as to pass the bucket.

To cut a long story short, Aesop's mission was to discover which animal had displeased the gods by its choice of menu. He would therefore ask each animal in turn to state what it last ate and say 'Good' or 'Bad' apparently at random. In fact, he would previously have picked on a common letter of the alphabet as 'taboo' and subsequently disapproved of all answers containing it. The object of the game would be, for those who knew it, to deduce what letter was currently taboo in order to avoid being disapproved of, or, for those who didn't, to wonder what on earth the whole thing was about and whether Mamma, Papa and Emily were as *compos mentis* as they liked to pretend.

The basic idea may be presented more simply, and quite suitably for children, in the following way.

Having secretly picked on a letter of the alphabet as taboo, Aesop asks of each player in turn a question requiring a one-word answer. If the answer contains the taboo letter, Aesop expresses disapproval and the respondent loses a life. The first to lose three lives is the overall loser and pays a forfeit.

Supposing T to be the outlawed letter, the sequence may begin:

> *Aesop* How old are you?
> *Answer* One hundred. (Good)
> *Aesop* Who is your favourite author?
> *Answer* Dickens. (Good)

Aesop Who was that lady I saw you with last night?
Answer My sister. (Bad)

and so on.

Kolodny's Game

Two or more players
Mainly for adults
Requires concentration

Also emanating from the book by Fixx, Kolodny's Game may
be described as inductive rather than deductive. If you know
Bob Abbott's card game Eleusis, or have read Martin Gardner
on the subject (see *More Mathematical Puzzles and Diversions*
in Penguin Books), further explanation should be unnecessary.
If not, I suppose it will do to say that an inductive game is one
in which you do not know the rules of movement, but have to
find out what they are by seeing what happens when you make
a move. In the long run the game is deductive in that your
object is to discover something hidden: induction is the mental
process by which this is achieved. (If I appear to be playing
with words, it is because I have never been entirely convinced
that the distinction is as significant as is made out.)

As originally described by David Greene Kolodny, the rule of
the game is simply to discover the rule of the game. To this end
you ask questions and are given Yes/No answers. The answer,
however, refers to the form of the question rather than its
content. Exactly how depends on the rule previously invented,
but not stated, by the person questioned.

For example, the rule could be that questions ending in
letters A to M are answered Yes, those ending in N to Z are
answered No. Hence:

Are you lyinG? – Yes.
Are you telling the trutH? – Yes.
Do you know what you're talking abouT? – No.

Other rules could relate to whether or not the question contained the word *you*, whether or not it was preceded by '*Er* . . .', whether or not it contained a verb, and so on. It can be fun to play, because questions are framed with a view to testing hypothesized rules as to their form rather than for any other reason, and may consequently extend over a wide range of more or less facetious subjects. And there are some questions whose Yes/No answer required by logic may gravely embarrass the respondent!

Part Two
Written Word Games

The Moving Finger writes; and, having writ,
Moves on; nor all thy Piety nor Wit
   Shall lure it back to cancel half a Line,
Nor all thy Tears wash out a Word of it.

FITZGERALD, *Ruba'iyat*

8 · *Compilations*

A number of frequently described word games merely consist in seeing who can compile the longest list of words having something in common, which is specified in advance. For example, who can find the most words which begin and end with the same letter, such as *AriA*, *BomB*, *CyniC*, et cetera?

A problem with most of these is that when you have played them once you have played them for all time, or at least for a period of living memory. To enable you to keep going along the same theme, some of the more obvious games of this type are listed below. You will doubtless be able to think of others. You could, in fact, play a sort of Dealer's Choice, where each player in turn either chooses one of the games below or invents a new type of list to be compiled.

Digrams

A small group of players
Adults and older children
A fairly light exercise

No, not diagrams. A digram is two consecutive letters in the same word. For example, WORD contains the three digrams WO, OR, RD. (It is not to be confused with a di*graph*, which is a special kind of digram – one used to express a single sound for which there is no separate letter, such as TH and NG in the word THING.)

Generally, the idea is to think of a digram and then see who can list the most words containing it. Specify NX, for instance, and ANXIETY may spring to mind. Care must be taken in choosing the combination required. Some digrams are so common that players could spend all night writing lists. Almost any digram containing A, E, I or O falls into this category. Others may look feasible – such as MT – but prove highly unrewarding in practice. A recommended rule of this game is that none of the listed words may begin or end with the stated digram, otherwise most or all players will find them easily enough and the competitiveness is that much reduced.

Here are some suitable digrams to be getting on with:

BD, CR (not at the start of a word, remember!), DU, FT, GL, HT (easier than it looks), LS, MU, NL, OE (prohibiting words ending in OES), PM.

A suitable method of scoring for this game is to count 2 for a word which only you have found and 1 each for the rest. If the digram was a difficult one, so that the total number of different words found by all the players put together is less than (say) ten, you might avoid ties by scoring the lengths of the words instead – i.e. 1 per letter instead of 1 or 2 per word. If it proved too easy, you might instruct players to stop listing when they reach 25 words, and give a bonus of (say) 10 points to the player or players who found (a) the longest word and (b) the earliest word – that is, the one which would be listed first in the dictionary.

An obvious wrinkle of this game is to discover the stated digram in compound words, where the first letter is the last one of the first half and the second the first of the second. Given HP, for instance, you should soon come up with TOOTHPASTE. For KH you might think of INKHORN, a word still quoted in books on phonetics to illustrate an aspirated K sound. (In these days of cartridge pens and felt-tips I can't believe that many people remember what an inkhorn originally was. As an alternative I offer a horrible fungus called STINKHORN.)

Trigrams

A small group of players
Adults and older children
A fairly light game

Yes, obviously, a trigram is three consecutive letters in one word, and you play the game as described above for digrams. The only problem here is thinking of suitable trigrams to work on. Here are some to be getting on with:

ASM, CAU, CTR, HIG, IVI, LLO, NQU, RGE, TTL, UST

Remember: they must appear inside a word, not at either end.

Prefixes

A small group of players
Mainly for adults
Can give rise to argument

See who can make the longest list of words starting with a given prefix, such as:

BE- as in *be-calm* (but not as in *bedspring*)
CON- as in *con-tainerization* (but not as in *conker*)
DIS- as in *dis-temper* (but not as in *dishcloth*)
EN- as in *en-gulf* (but not as in *enough*)
FOR- as in *for-bid* (but not as in *fortnight*)
FORE- as in *fore-see* (but not as in *foreign*)
MIS- as in *mis-appropriate* (but not as in *mistletoe*)
PRE- as in *pre-caution* (but not as in *preen*)
SUB- as in *sub-marine* (but not as in *suberose* (= corky))
TRI- as in *tri-angle* (but not as in *tripwire*)

I think this is a silly game, but there's no accounting for taste. Don't play it if you don't understand why some of the words listed above are allowable and others are not. The best prefixes are FOR- and FORE-, as they throw up the players who don't know the difference between FORBEAR and FORE-BEAR, and who commit the common error of writing FORSEE instead of FORESEE. But don't be too hard on anyone who writes DISLEXIA instead of DYSLEXIA. There may be a good reason for it.

Suffixes

Any number of players
Adults and older children
A light game

This is like Prefixes, only at the other end. English suffixes include -MENT, -SHIP, -LESS, -NESS, and even -LESSNESS, but as there are so many of each it would be reasonable to impose some other restriction, such as that they should all begin with the same letter. (Not necessarily the same letter for each player: they could be allowed to choose their own.)

Not strictly a suffix is the Latin word-root CEDE, as in PRECEDE, INTERCEDE and so on. But it might be fun to put it in, just to see how many players come up with one of the commonest spelling mistakes of our time, namely SUPERCEDE for SUPERSEDE.

Fore and Aft

Any number of players
Any age, but do not mix abilities
A very light game

So called by Mr Brandreth, this game has as its object to find as many words as possible which begin and end with the same letter. To give it quality as well as quantity, you may like to add the following rules:

1. Only one word is required for each letter.

2. The player or players who find the longest word for a given letter score(s) an extra point for it. To break ties between different words of equal length, the point goes to the word which comes first in the dictionary.

Head to Tail

A small group of players
Adults and older children
A more demanding game

State a two-word compound, such as FLAPJACK, JACK-KNIFE, KNIFE RACK, etc. (As you can see, it doesn't matter if the two words are written separately, together or in hyphenation, so long as they go together with a distinctive meaning.) Then see who, in the space of (say) two minutes, can write the longest chain of compounds such that the first word of each is the last word of the one preceding.

As an example, the chain started above might continue RACK-RAIL, RAILWAY, WAYSIDE, SIDEBOARD, BOARD GAME, GAME-BIRD, and so on.

A real *tour de force* would be to go for the longest circular chain, but for this purpose you must choose the first compound carefully. Off-hand I can't think of a compound ending in -FLAP to bring us back to FLAPJACK in the illustration above, but one of the later words might work, such as WAYSIDE. (I have just thought of PUSS-FLAP, an English cat-lover's term for a hinged flap in a doorway to enable pet cats to come and go.)

Bacronyms

Any number of players
Adults and older children
A fairly light game

A palindrome is a word that reads the same backwards as forwards, such as MADAM. A homonym is a word with two different meanings – or, more accurately, two different words that have the same form, such as *stick* ('rod' or 'adhere'). What do you call a word which is the same as a different word spelt backwards, such as W A R D and D R A W? The word 'semordnilap' has been suggested. A nice idea, but it doesn't really work being hardly pronounceable and in any case inconsistent with the pattern of English. I prefer to call such words 'bacronyms', largely as a gesture of defiance to those who seem to think there is something not quite nice about mixing word roots from different languages. (I wonder what word they use instead of *television*.)

Having said that (as they say, having said it) I have little to offer beyond a game in which the object is to compile the longest possible list of bacronyms you can find. In case this seems an endless task, or formless, as the case may be, discipline can be imposed by specifying (a) word length, e.g. find as many four-letter bacronyms as you can, then progressively raise the number on subsequent rounds of play; and/or (b) initial letters, e.g. find as many bacronyms as you can beginning with . . . whatever it may be. I would avoid as initials the letters J, K, Q, U, V, X, Z.

Sequences

Any number of players
Adults and older children
Requires thought

List as many words as you can find which contain (a) two consecutive letters of the alphabet, e.g. alphABet, then (b) three consecutive, e.g. DEFy, then (c) four consecutive letters, such as . . . well, there must be one, mustn't there?

A variation on this would be to list words whose letters all fall within a particular range of the alphabet, such as all the letters up to but not beyond J, and so on.

And if you have not yet looked at the list on page 225, you might like to see how many words can be found whose only vowel is Y. I must say that I discovered more than I would have expected.

Stairway

Any number of players
Any age, but do not mix abilities
As competitive as you care to make it

One of several listing games described by Gyles Brandreth, Stairway is more interesting than it sounds at first hearing.

A letter is chosen at random and a time limit announced, say five minutes. At the end of that time the winner is the player who has compiled the longest list of words beginning with it, such that the first is a word of two letters, the second of three, the third of four, and so on, increasing by one letter at a time.

To prevent ties or otherwise add interest, a player may score an additional point for a word of any given length which comes earliest in the dictionary – e.g. one player's BAD would beat another's BAG, scoring 2 to the latter's 1 point.

Obviously, a break in the stairway ends the list – no gaps are allowed.

Beheadings

Any number of players
Mainly for adults
Quite challenging

This game does not work very often, since there is a best possible result, but it makes a nice competition for people who haven't come across it before.

The object of the game is to list twenty-six words starting with successive letters of the alphabet and having the property that, when beheaded, the remains form another valid word. For example, ARID, beheaded, becomes RID; BLOOM, beheaded, LOOM.

The real competition lies in seeing who can produce, on

average, the longest words of this type. For this purpose each player scores 1 point for each letter of the words remaining after beheadment – thus ARID to RID scores 3 points, and so on.

My source for this game is the American National Puzzlers League. Counting only words found as main entries in the *Merriam-Webster Pocket Dictionary*, the highest possible score is given as 199, the best result achieved in actual competition conditions being 129. The words producing the record result are listed on page 227, although not all twenty-six initial letters can be represented – two are lacking.

Owing to differences of spelling between opposite sides of the Atlantic the target for British players is 200 rather than 199. Also, one of the words in the American list does not work when transposed into British spelling, and I have accordingly replaced it with another word of equal length which (for Americans) may not appear in *Merriam-Webster*.

The game can be varied in several ways. One is to score for the shortest possible beheadments. Another is to reward the player who compiles his list first, provided that he is not subsequently beaten by a longer list. Another is to reward only words ending in a given letter, containing a given letter or being of a given length.

Numwords

Any number of players
Adults and older children
Quite challenging

I have based several word games and puzzles on the idea of considering words as numbers – hence 'numwords' – in the following way. Count A as 1, B as 2, and so on up to Z as 26. A numword of value N is then defined as a word whose constituent letters total N under this system. The value itself may be called a 'wordnum'. Thus the wordnum of the numword THING would be 58, i.e. $20 + 8 + 9 + 14 + 7$. For games based on this principle, apart from the listing game about to be described, see Centurion and Inflation.

The listing game is quite simple. A number is selected at random and a time-limit quoted, say two minutes. The winner is the player who by the end of that time has produced the longest list of numwords having exactly that value. Extra credit may be given for producing (a) the shortest and (b) the longest word discovered.

Since the average value of a letter is 13½, somewhere between 65 and 70 would be a suitable value to suggest if, on average, five-letter words are envisaged.

Variant: For a given length of word, or for a given initial letter, see who can find (a) the lowest and (b) the highest valued numword meeting the specification. For example, the lowest three-letter numword is ABB, worth 5; the highest acceptable to me would be WRY, worth 66.

Categories and Guggenheim

Any number of players
Any age, but do not mix abilities
A quietly competitive game

One thing I discovered during my teaching days was that children of all ages adore general-knowledge quizzes – by which, if it is left to them to set the questions, they mean highly specialized knowledge, and the more arcane or esoteric, the better. And since 'children of all ages' includes adults, it is hardly surprising that Categories has remained a perennially favourite family game since Victoria's days and possibly even earlier. (It is also known as Guggenheim, but I regard this as a variant and will come back to it later.) If any excuse is needed for including a general-knowledge exercise in a book of word games, it is that all the emphasis is placed on the words used to convey the knowledge in question.

Basic method of play A set of category headings – twenty is a suitable number – is agreed on by the players, each of whom writes them in a list down the left-hand side of a piece of paper. Typical category headings might include Town, Bird, Actor, Clothing and so on, but we will go into details later.

A letter of the alphabet is then selected at random, such as by drawing a lettered card or tile from a boxed game, or by taking a book, choosing a page number at random, and taking the first letter printed on that page. Letters Q, X and Z tend to make for a dull game and should be avoided, while children may not be happy with J, K, U, V or Y either.

A time limit is set, say 10 minutes. During that period each player tries to find an example of each category which begins with the letter in question. For example, initial A might produce the following:

Town Aberdeen
Bird Albatross
Actor Asher (Jane)
Clothing Anorak

When the time is up, each person passes their paper to the left for marking. The examples given for each category are read out and a point scored for each one. It may well happen that a particular answer is queried or challenged as to acceptability. For instance, as a game beginning with A, would you accept 'American football'? Probably so amongst British players, for whom it differs from the game they know simply as football, but not amongst American players, for whom the word 'American' is unnecessary. The rule I recommend for such queries is that an answer is acceptable if at least one opponent accepts it, but not if they unanimously reject it.

The winner is obviously the player who scores most points. Equally obviously, the game may continue with the selection of another initial letter for the same twenty categories.

Now let's look at some sample categories and ways of varying the basic game for perhaps greater interest or challenge.

Choosing the categories The simplest way of choosing a set of categories is to let each player in turn nominate one and to forbid it if everyone else objects to it. The player who suggested the rejected category does not get a second turn until it comes round to him again in the normal course of events. This should overcome the irritation of being forced into esoteric subjects. (I only accept Footballer if I am allowed Language, and Rock Group if I can have Heavenly Body, by which I mean astronomical object rather than . . . well, fill it in yourself.)

I offer the following list of sample categories just to set your mind running along suitable tracks. They are pretty general, as befits a circle of players of mixed ages or abilities, but can be restricted or split into other categories as suggested in parentheses after each one.

PEOPLE BY NAME
Actor/actress/film star/TV celebrity
Artist (Painter, Sculptor, Photographer, Cartoonist, etc.)
Fictitious Character (or Legendary, Mythical, etc.)
Historical Character (King, Queen, Head of State, Hero/ Heroine, etc.)
Musician (Composer, Conductor, Performer, Rock Group, etc.)
Politician
Saint
Scientist
Sportsperson (Footballer, Cricketer, Swimmer, Runner, Commentator, etc.)
Writer (Novelist, Poet, Playwright, Journalist, etc.)

Answers to these categories should use the letter chosen as the initial of the surname or name by which listed in an index. John Wayne, for instance, would do for W but not for J, though I would accept Napoleon Buonaparte under N or B.

Some agreement should be reached beforehand as to the extent to which examples of these categories may be living only or living-or-dead and whether or not they may be of any nationality.

I am not happy with the categories Boy's Name and/or Girl's

Name, having been put off by the discovery that one of the
Beatles (I think it was) named his son Zak. And people who
live on the opposite side of the Atlantic from myself do tend to
go in for nonce-names, nonce-spellings and abbreviations such
as Barbra, Stu, de Forest and others, which raise complications as to acceptability. It is for this reason, rather than for
any overtly Catholic propensity, that we replaced this category
by 'Saint', though even here we have had to ban long lists of
obscure Welsh 'saints' which can more or less be produced by
randomizing almost any set of alphabetical characters.

PERSONAL CONCEPTS
Clothing, item of, including item of adornment
Food, item of
Illness or Disease
Nationality
Occupation

NATURAL WORLD
Animal (Mammal, Reptile/Amphibian, Dinosaur, etc.)
Bird
Fish (or any other underwater creature)
Insect (or any other invertebrate)
Plant (Flower, Tree, Shrub, Fruit, Vegetable, etc.)

In this set of categories agreement should be reached as to
whether or not extinct examples are allowed, or a separate
category of Extinct Animals may be introduced.

GEOGRAPHICAL
Country
Mountain
River
Town/City
Water, body of

Some of these need comment. By Country, for example, do
you mean necessarily an independent state such as the United
Kingdom, or will you accept principalities such as Wales and

Categories and Guggenheim 97

autonomous regions such as Nakhichevan Autonomous
Republic of the Azerbaijan Soviet Socialist Republic? What
about Catalonia, Palestine, Utopia, the Byzantine Empire and
Gondwanaland?

Mountains rarely give rise to arguments, but rivers can raise
contributory problems.

Towns are vexatious since there is no unarguable dividing
line between a small town and a large village. Bodies of water
are less arguable, though also less easy to think of. This
category includes oceans, seas, lakes and lochs but probably
falls short of the ponds on Tooting Bec Common, where I
spent many a happy childhood day.

A related category, if you want to be clever, is Geographical
Phenomena, such as *desert*, *moraine*, *glacier*, *strata* and suchlike.

MISCELLANEOUS
Game (for playing, not bagging)
Heavenly Body (e.g. star, asteroid, Pluto, Betelgeuse, etc.)
Language (excluding body language, foul language, etc.)
Liquid (not necessarily potable: e.g. mercury)
Means of Transport (excluding transports of delight, etc.)
Railway Station (especially, for Londoners, Underground
    stations)
Title of book, play, film, opera, etc. (argue among your-
    selves)
Tool or Implement (ditto)
Unit of Measurement (and/or Currency)
Weapon (intended as such, as opposed to umbrella)

Time limit You may wish to ignore the race element of
Categories by dropping the specified time limit. My suggestion
for this is that everyone announces when they are ready for
marking, but may continue trying to fill gaps until all but one
player have said they are ready, at which point the time is up.

Alternatively, you may emphasize the race element by
having the players hand their papers in to a central point when

they are ready, and crediting (say) an extra 3 points to the first, 2 to the second and 1 to the third to do so.

Scoring Many players feel that credit should be given for coming up with obscure rather than common answers. One way of doing this is as follows: if, for any given category, everybody comes up with the same answer *or* a different answer (i.e. either all the same or no duplicates), they score 1 each. If two players share an answer they score half each; three score a third each, and so on. If you don't like messing around with fractions, score a basic 12 for each one and divide by the number of duplicates. Or score 1 per player less 1 per duplicate.

A neater method of achieving a similar effect is proposed by Richard Sharp: each in turn reads his list out; anyone else who has the same answer for the same category sticks his hand up; the reader scores 1 point for each hand that doesn't go up.

Another way of increasing the interest of the score is to give a bonus point to the player or players who come up with the *shortest* word for a given category.

In *Guggenheim*, each player draws a grid of (say) 5 × 5 squares. Down the left-hand side go five agreed categories, and five different letters go along the top. The rest is as before – i.e., you play five short games of Categories at once.

Word Ladders

Any number of players
Any age
Fun and competitive

A perennial favourite. Two words of the same length are agreed, and the winner is the first to construct a ladder converting one to the other by changing only one letter at a time. (If preferred, the shortest ladder wins.) For example, using only words listed in my nearest dictionary, I can get from ABBA to ZOON in sixteen steps: ABBA, ABBE, ABLE, ABLY, ALLY, ILLY, INLY, ONLY, OILY, WILY, WILE, BILE, BOLE, BORE, BORN, BOON, ZOON. (Can you do better?)

In-words is short for words-within-words, by analogy with wheels-within-wheels, and makes a good heading for some of the simplest but cleverest of all word games and puzzles. Given a word, how many other words can you make out of it, using only those letters contained in the given word but not necessarily all of them? THEM, for instance, gives you EH, EM, HEM, HET, ME, MET, TE and THE, so think what you can do with a word like CONTEMPORANEOUSLY.

When I say 'cleverest', I mean that such games sort out the players with the biggest vocabularies and quickest sifting processes. Truth to tell, they are not really games so much as competitions, in that each player works by himself at the problem and has no way of influencing or interacting with the other players. But there is a 'winner' to the extent that scores can be given for producing the most or best words, and the ages of silent contemplation are more than made up for by the period of reading lists and comparing notes, when players can be heard kicking themselves for failing to spot fairly simple words that everyone else has got.

Word Hunt

or Words within Words, Key Words, Target, etc.

Any number of players
Any age
A quietly competitive exercise

Yes, it's that game where you see who can make the longest list of words using only letters found in a given key word. My gaming group went through a craze and played it into the ground several years ago. It even got to the stage where we gave ourselves a whole week in which to glean words by any amount of brain- or dictionary-racking that we could find time and inclination for; but, looking back on it, I think this could justifiably be regarded as taking it to excess.

For some years now a variation on it has been run in the *Daily Express* under the title Target. In this you are given nine letters in a 3 × 3 box. The main object is to make at least as many words as the targets set for different levels (e.g., 25 words 'average', 30 words 'excellent'); as a nice disciplinary touch, every word must include the letter in the centre of the box and your list must contain at least one nine-letter word.

I lost patience with Target after a while, especially for its silly rule forbidding plurals. I think the intention is to prevent padding by cutting out words taking a grammatical ending in S, in which case the best way of doing it is to avoid giving as the nine-letter key word any one containing S in the first place. As it is, the stated rule theoretically forbids such words as *data*, *mice* and so on (though I am sure I have seen *data* given in one of its solutions) and theoretically does not forbid such third-person singular verb forms as *goes*, though whenever I claim such words they turn out not to be included in the solution.

How to play Word Hunt is one of the few word games in which four or five is a better number of players than two or three. It should be played with a time limit, which may vary from five minutes to half an hour, depending on the length of the key word and the degree of competitiveness to which it is played.

Each player is equipped with pencil and paper and sat somewhere un-overlookable. A key word is selected more or less at random, from memory or from a book. From eight to twelve letters is a suitable length of word.

Within the time available, each player must write as long a list as possible of words which can be made from the key word. That is, each listed word must be composed only of letters found in the key word. A letter appearing only once in the key word may be used only once in each list word; one appearing twice may be used not more than twice, and so on. ('One-to-one correspondence' is the official rule, translated into jargon.)

It is usual to agree that list words should be at least four letters in length, but when children are playing this may be reduced to three; you may also want to impose an upper limit on length. It is also reasonable to discount appearances of the same word with different grammatical endings, e.g. if you list TALK you may not also count TALKS or TALKED; this does not exclude fundamentally different forms of words which are etymologically the same, such as SEEK and SOUGHT. You may also have words with a grammatical -S in order to reach the minimum permitted word length. For example, LAY may be unacceptable because the minimum permitted length is four letters, but LAYS will then be allowed. Words such as MORE and MORES count as two, since the latter, in the sense of 'customs' or 'manners', differs in both form and meaning from the former. (It would be ridiculous, though, to count homonyms more than once – e.g., WAKE is only one word even though it has two quite unconnected meanings.) The usual restrictions may be imposed on proper names and foreign, obsolete or hyphenated words.

The game may be ended and scored to taste. As soon as an agreed time is up, finish writing your last word. The player with the longest claimed list reads it out and everyone ticks off the words they have, supplying in addition any others they have which were omitted by the first player. Disputed words must be settled by any agreed method. The player with the longest list wins. Or, as a refinement, score 1 point for words shared with other players, 2 for a word shared with only one other player, and 5 for any acceptable word which only you managed to find.

Acrosticals

Two or more players
Adults and older children
Competitive, but amusing

First described by Gyles Brandreth under the rather undistinctive title Dictionary, Acrosticals is basically a variation on Word Hunt (above) but is far too good to be relegated to a tailpiece to that game. It is currently my group's favourite word game, and we played a session of it last night to provide some examples and statistics for the following account.

How to play Select a word of ten letters, preferably without too many duplications of the same letter. The first one we came up with last night was PERSIFLAGE, so I will take this as an example. Each player writes the word vertically down the left-hand side of his paper.

The object is to compile a list of 10 words, each of which uses only letters contained in the key word on a one-to-one basis (as in Word Hunt). The first word must begin with P, the second with E, and so on throughout the keyword PERSIFLAGE or whatever it may be. Only one word is needed for each letter, though if any letters are repeated (in this case E) the two words based on that initial must be different. The first word in the list must not be another but shorter relative of the key word; e.g., if the key word were DICTIONARY your first word could not acceptably be DICTION. The most important point is that you score according to the length of words you can make – the longer, the better.

There are several ways of finishing. We merely wait until all players are agreed that they cannot get any further, but as alternatives you can play for a fixed amount of time (say ten or fifteen minutes), or else stop as soon as one player says 'Stop', provided that the stopper has completed 10 words.

The players then announce their words, scoring 1 point per letter for each word if acceptable within the rules of play.

Theoretically, the maximum possible score is 100, obtainable only if ten different anagrams can be found of the original key word! Some key words prove easier than others, but our experience is that 60 is a good average target score, with a practical achievement range of 50 to 70.

Here are our four results for PERSIFLAGE:

PRESAGE	7	PLEASE	6	PILFERS	7	PRAISE	6
ELAPSE	6	EARS	4	EAGLES	6	EAGLES	6
RELAPSE	7	RIFLES	6	REGALES	7	REPLIES·	7
SERIF	5	SPIRAL	6	SPIRAL	6	SILAGE	6
IRE	3	ISLE	4	IFS	3	ISLE	4
FRAIL	5	FLARES	6	FRAGILE	7	FRAGILE	7
LARGE	5	LAGERS	6	LAGERS	6	LAGERS	6
ARISE	5	AGREES	6	AGILE	5	ASPIRE	6
GRAPES	6	GRAPES	6	GRAPES	6	GRAILS	6
EAGLES	6	ERASE	5	ERASE	5	ERASE	5

Score:	55		55		58		59

It's quite surprising that two fairly literate people failed to get ISLE out of the key word, one of them being me. IFS is quite acceptable, of course: there are no ifs and buts about it. Our average score was 56·75, but the best possible score – if we assume it to be that of all the highest-scoring words in the four lists – works out at 61.

Here are four more key words which we used for the purpose of illustrating Acrosticals. In each case I will give you our actual scores and the best possible score on the basis of those figures. See if you can beat our 'best possibles' before turning to the list of best words given on page 228.

CUSTOMABLE scored 54, 57, 58, 62. Best: 65
PNEUMATICS scored 54, 56, 61, 62. Best: 67
CENTRALITY scored 63, 64, 68, 68. Best: 74

Name in Vain

Any number of players
Mainly for adults
Amusing rather than competitive, but much thought needed

Much amusement is to be earned through deriving anagrams from well-known names – the pithier, the better. Stock examples include:

FLORENCE NIGHTINGALE: Flit on, cheering angel.
ROBERT LOUIS STEVENSON: Our best novelist, señor.
ADOLF HITLER: Hated for ill.
PIET MONDRIAN: I paint modern.
CLINT EASTWOOD: Old West action.
WESTERN UNION: No wire unsent.
MARGARET THATCHER: That great charmer.
MARGARET THATCHER: Great harm, her act.

To turn this into a game, simply agree on a name and see who first comes up with a workable anagram on it.

More elaborately, set a ten-minute time limit on each one. The winner is the player whose anagram is voted best by the others. (No one may vote for their own.) Before the ten minutes is up, anyone may claim that no sensible anagram is possible. In this event, either the claimant wins, if no one has produced one within the allotted period, or else the first player to produce one after the challenge.

10 · *Sequentials*

Sequentials have already been introduced as a class of spoken word games; those that follow are the written equivalents. Under this heading are grouped games in which each player in turn adds a new word to a list in such a way as to match or continue the theme of those that have gone before, or to reduce the number of words available for the next player to make or claim. They do not all conform exactly to this description, but the essence of all the games is the same following-on procedure. On the whole, they are more competitive and challenging than many other games in the book, including sequentials of the spoken variety.

Uncrash

Two to four players
Adults and older children
A quite fast and light game

Ross Eckler is my source for the following game, which he described (in *Games & Puzzles* magazine) in conjunction with the deductive games of Jotto and Crash. Although obviously derived from them, however, Uncrash is not a deductive game, fitting instead into the 'following-on' group.

A written list of words is gradually built up, for which purpose either one list can be kept, each player in turn writing the next additional word to it, or else each player can keep his own written list, with each in turn stating what the next word is to be. The second method is more comfortable.

The game is played with an agreed length of word, say three

letters. The first player states or writes a starting word, let us say: SAY.

The second then writes underneath it a word containing no crashes with the first one – that is to say, it may not begin with S or end with Y or have A in the middle. For example: NOT.

This continues with each player adding a three-letter word which must contain no crashes with any word that has gone before. The first player unable to play without crashing is the loser, and/or the last to add a word to the list is the winner.

A four-player game might run as follows:

1. SAY
2. NOT
3. AHA
4. ONE
1. PUB
2. FIX
3. YEW
4. GYP
1. EGG
2. IRK
3. TWO
4. ?

The fourth player loses because he cannot find a continuation which does not crash with a previous word (even if you can), so the third player wins.

What always fascinates me about games of this type – where the winner is the last one able to play – is the possibility of using post mortems to spot the losing move. Evidently the fourth player's word GYP was a losing move. What could he have entered instead which would produce a more favourable result? Or, if you emphasize the fact that the third player has won, then the second player's IRK was a losing move. What better word could he have come up with?

Uncrash can be played with words of any agreed length. The greater the length, the longer, on average, will a series last before someone crashes. Obviously no game can last longer than twenty-six moves.

One way of increasing the scope without getting too complicated is to play as follows: words of five, seven or nine letters are entered in such a way as to ensure that individual letters fall into clearly defined columns. Crashing is then judged only on the central three, five or seven letters, which, of course, need not be words.

You can turn it into a solitaire, i.e. make a puzzle or challenge out of it, by trying to discover (a) the shortest and (b) the longest sequence of words that can possibly be produced from a format of any given length.

Word Ping-Pong

Two or more players
Adults and older children
Light-hearted but lengthy

One of the few word games with a format based on something else (the only others that spring to mind are Hangman and the Number Plate Game), Word Ping-Pong is a form of competitive word ladders invented by P. Perkins and first published in *Games & Puzzles* magazine.

It helps to know that Ping-Pong or Table Tennis is played up to 21 points, with each player serving (going first) five times in succession – i.e. whenever the two players' individual scores sum to a multiple of five, it is time for the other player to start serving. The winner is the first to reach 21, but if a score of 20-20 is reached the service alternates and the winner is the first to gain a 2-point lead. A rally is a period of play starting with a service and ending with the score of a point.

Decide who serves first by any agreed means. Service is made by writing down a word of four letters. This starts a list, which is continued by each player in turn. Each word on the list must differ from the preceding word by one letter. The server may change only the first or second letter of the word, his opponent only the third or fourth. The first word (service) must be convertible by a third or fourth letter change, otherwise the server's opponent scores. The same word may not appear twice in one rally, nor the same service twice in one game. Neither player may use the same letter in the same position more than three times in one rally. A rally ends when one player is unable to continue, whereupon his opponent scores a point.

Perkins's illustration of a rally runs thus:

1. LAST
2. LAS*H*
3. *C*ASH
4. CAS*T*
5. *P*AST
6. PA*N*T
7. P*I*NT
8. PIN*E*
9. *W*INE
10. WI*S*E
11. *R*ISE
12. RICE

The server, playing odd numbers in the list above, cannot continue. He has already used A and I each three times in the same position and may not use either for a fourth, and there are no such words as RECE, ROCE or RYCE. His opponent therefore scores, and the server starts again.

Four people may play 'doubles', i.e. in partnerships of two against two. On each side the partners play alternately, and they may not confer. Neither partnership may use the same letter three times in the same position.

The game for three or more   Three or more may play in this way.

Each writes a four-letter word in turn, which must differ from the preceding word by one letter. No player may change either of the letters introduced by the two previous players. No letter may appear more than five times in any one position.

When a player cannot continue, he scores a penalty point and the next takes over. If no one can continue, the rally is at an end and the turn to serve passes to the left of the previous server. (If all pass except the player who last wrote a word, the latter may add another to the list if he can – thus opening it up into play again – but does not score a penalty if unable to do so.)

Play up to any agreed target or for any agreed number of rounds. The winner is the player with the fewest penalty points.

Nymphabet

Two players
Adults and older children
A fast game unless played seriously

I devised this game as an alphabetical version of Nim, whence its title. Nim, which appears in many forms, is any game of a type in which each player in turn removes, takes away or otherwise 'nims' (an old English term) a number of objects, the winner being the one who takes the last object – or who forces his opponent to do so. Nymphabet may be played and scored in several different ways, in case you should find that any one of them leads to a forced win for either player.

The simplest version is played as follows. Write out the alphabet from A to Z. Each player in turn writes a word in accordance with the following rules, and the person who writes the last word is the loser. The first word must begin with A, which is duly crossed off the alphabet as having been 'used'. If it also contains a B, the B is deleted; if it also contains a C somewhere *following* the B, C is deleted. So is any D following the C, and so on. For example, the first word might be ALL, deleting A; or ABLE, deleting A and B; or ABACK, deleting A, B and C; or ABDICATED, deleting all four letters from A to D. (Note that ABDICATE alone only deletes up to C, because the D comes before it and therefore does not count.)

The second player's first word must begin with the next

letter of the alphabet yet to be deleted. As before, any letters
consecutive to it are deleted provided that they occur in correct
sequence in the word.

Here is a sample game:

1st player	2nd player
ABaCk	DEFyinG
HIJacK	LaMiNatiOn
PiQue	ReSTaUrant
VoW	XYlophone
Zip (*loses*)	

Played this way, the game is rather more interesting if the
writer of the last word loses. After a while, you will discover
that the player whose word contains U as its last deletion wins
the game (unless the other can find a word beginning with V
that also eliminates W and X, since V alone loses after WAXY
is played as the next word). Further backtracking along these
lines shows that whoever eliminates up to P wins, for whatever
is played next he will be able to eliminate up to U again (unless
there is a Q-word which also eliminates R, S, T and U – I
haven't found one yet).

When you have carried out further researches of this nature
and discovered that one player has an inbuilt advantage, you
will look for ways of opening up the game again. For instance:

Variation 1 The first way is to treat the alphabet as circular –
that is, with A following in sequence from Z. The game is
played as before, except that (a) the first player may begin
anywhere in the alphabet and (b) the winner is the last to
complete a word. Thus:

1st player	2nd player
MeNtiOn	PiQue
ReSTaUrant	VoW
XYlem	ZeAl
BaCkeD	EFfiGy
HIp	JacKaL (*wins*)

Variation 2 The game may be played starting at any letter as in Variation 1, but this time the win is determined not by who does or does not write the last word but by whoever makes the larger score. This is found by noting after each word the number of letters it deletes, and finally multiplying together all the scores made by one player. For example:

1st player		2nd player	
QueeReST	4	UVula	2
WaXY	3	ZABaglione	3
CeDE	3	FiGHtIng	4
JacKaL	3	MiNOrshiP	4

The first player scores $4 \times 3 \times 3 \times 3 = 108$, the second $2 \times 3 \times 4 \times 4 = 96$. Had the second written UnVoWed, he might have won by 192 to 96. The game can be played up to 1000 points.

(I have met word-gamers who pretend that multiplication is beyond their powers, which strikes me as a form of inverted snobbery. You could add the scores instead of multiplying and agree that in the event of equality the win goes to the player who went second.)

Arrow of Letters or Verbal Sprouts

Two players
Adults and elderly children
Can get complicated

This unusual and clever word game was invented by Michael Grendon and first published in *Games & Puzzles*. Its alternative title may show how it is derived from a well-known abstract pencil-and-paper game.

On plain paper rather than ruled, each player in turn writes a letter within a circle, in a straight line, until a four-letter word has been made. The four letters must be different and they must form a word, but at this stage neither player has an advantage and there is no point in trying to think strategically ahead. A starting position for a game may therefore look like this:

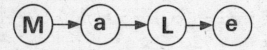

I have used capitals for the first player and small letters for the second, but this is only for illustration and not essential to the game. The opening diagram is completed by connecting the circled letters with arrowed lines, as illustrated.

From now on, each player in turn adds a new letter in a circle, and connects it by means of arrows to one or more existing letters. The new letter must be different from any previous letter in the diagram (thus preventing the game from going on for ever). The player then scores, at the rate of 1 point per letter, for each word he can make which uses the letter he entered and correctly follows the line of arrows he has drawn.

For example, to the above diagram the first player might add the letter T and appropriate arrows like this:

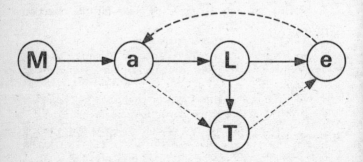

From this he can form the new words MALT, MATE and TEAL for a score of 12.

His opponent could then continue with an R and suitable arrows thus:

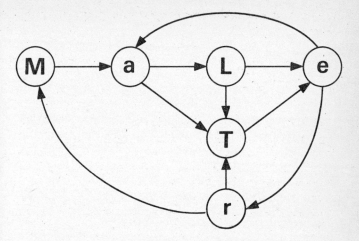

This gives him 4 for TERM plus 5 for ALERT, making 9 in all.

Play continues in this way until neither player can move, at which point the winner is the one with the higher score.

The following additional rules apply:

1. Words may only be made by following the direction indicated by the arrows.
2. Arrows may not cross one another.
3. No encircled letter may be attached to more than four arrows (whether by point or by flight), but a four-arrowed letter may still be used in subsequent words.
4. No given pair of letters may be connected by more than one arrow, and that arrow may follow one direction only.
5. A shorter word may not be entirely contained within a longer. For example, the score for MATE and TEAL in the first example may not be increased by scores for ATE and TEA.

Mr Grendon points out that the rule which allows players only to score for words containing the letter they have just entered prevents one player from profiting by any that his opponent may have overlooked, and observes: 'There is room for an optional variant here.' Such a variant would be a rule equivalent to 'huffing' in the game of Draughts, whereby a player could claim anything his opponent fails to score.

It is not clear whether the prohibition on scoring for shorter words contained in longer applies to words of equal length obtained by reading from different positions. For instance, if a given word were LANE, would it be permissible to join E to L and score in the same turn for ELAN? I think this should be permitted.

Centurion

Two or more players
Adults and older children
Requires concentration

If you have no head for figures and don't like adding up, try this game of my invention. It will do you good.

The main game is for two players.

The letters of the alphabet are assigned numerical values corresponding to their positions in the alphabet: i.e. A = 1, B 2, C 3, D 4, E 5, F 6, G 7, H 8, I 9, J 10, K 11, L 12, M 13, N 14, O 15, P 16, Q 17, R 18, S 19, T 20, U 21, V 22, W 23, X 24, Y 25, Z 26.

The first player writes down a three-letter word whose combined numerical value is 10 or under, e.g.:

ACE = 9 (1 + 3 + 5)

The second writes under it a three-letter word beginning with the last letter of the first and beside it notes the cumulative total of letters written so far, e.g.:

END = 32 (5 + 14 + 4 added to the 9 for ACE)

This continues, each adding a three-letter word beginning with the last letter of the previous word and writing the total beside it. No word may appear more than once in the list.

The player whose word causes the total to reach three figures is the loser. The game started above might continue as follows:

DAB adds 7 for 39
BUG adds 30 for 69
GOD adds 26 for 95

Since the lowest-valued continuation is DAD, worth 9, the next player cannot go without 'busting', and loses.

Double Centurion is played in the same way but by three or more players and up to a losing target of 200. Four may play in partnerships, playing in rotation and without consultation.

Inflation

Two or more players
Adults and older children
Requires concentration

A close relative of Centurion, Inflation is based on the same principle of assigning values to the letters of the alphabet, from A = 1 to Z = 26.

The first player writes down a three-letter word whose total letter value is not more than 10, together with its actual value, e.g.:

ACE = 9

This starts a list. Each in turn then adds a three-letter word to it and writes its total word value after it (not the cumulative total as in Centurion). Each new word must start with a letter taken from the previous word, and no word may be used twice in the same list.

The point of the game is that each new word must also be higher in value than the one before it. A player who cannot add a higher-valued word to the list is the loser.

The shortest possible game lasts three moves, with several possibilities for the first two words:

ABB = 5
BOW = 40
WRY = 64

Since WRY is the highest-valued three-letter word acceptable under my rules of play, anyone who enters a word containing W is giving the game away.

Oilers

Two players
Adults and older children
Requires concentration, but quite fast

If I mention that the name of this game is connected in a roundabout way with the mathematician Euler (pronounced 'Oiler'), you will then not be surprised to discover that it is not really a word game but rather a mathematical game which happens to make use of a set of words. In fact, Oilers eventually proves to be Noughts and Crosses, or Tic Tac Toe, thinly disguised as a word game. It was first described in the magazine *Word Ways* by Dave Silverman, and appears in two forms – simple and advanced.

For the simple game there is a stockpile of nine four-letter words. These may be written in a list and one crossed off at each move, or written on separate slips and one drawn at each move. Essentially, therefore, each move consists in 'capturing' a word. The nine words are:

FISH	SOUP	SWAN
GIRL	HORN	ARMY
KNIT	VOTE	CHAT

Each player in turn takes a word. The winner is the first to take three words sharing a letter in common. If neither achieves this object, the result is a draw. Suppose, for example, words are taken as follows:

Arnold HORN
Byron SOUP
Arnold KNIT
Byron SWAN (otherwise Arnold has three Ns)
Arnold FISH (otherwise Byron has three S's)
Byron GIRL
Arnold CHAT (*wins*)

Arnold has captured all three words containing an H. Had Byron attempted to prevent it by taking CHAT instead of GIRL, Arnold would have taken GIRL and won with three Is.

My reference to Noughts and Crosses and the way in which the nine given words are arranged on the page now clearly show how 'trivial' the game is, in the sense that, with best possible play, the result is always a draw. You will note that each row, column and diagonal of three words is characterized by the common possession of one letter – S in the top row, for example, or H in the top left to bottom right diagonal. The capture of a word, therefore, whether by crossing off a list or drawing a slip, is precisely equivalent to placing a distinctive mark in any of the nine spaces of the grid. Arnold wins because, knowing that the game is essentially Noughts and Crosses, he takes first the one word – HORN – containing letters common to four lines and so equivalent to the centre space. Byron loses because, not being aware of this fact, he in effect places his first mark on a middle edge, a well-known losing move.

More interesting than this, however, is the advanced game. The advanced game is played with a stockpile of sixteen three-letter words, namely:

APE	DAY	CAN	RAT
LIP	DIE	TIN	RIG
HOP	DOT	ONE	ROW
PUT	BUD	SUN	RUE

At each turn a player 'takes' a word. The first to move – the 'toiler' – wins if *either* player gathers four words sharing a letter in common. His opponent – the 'spoiler' – wins if *neither* of them achieves this result by the time all sixteen words have been taken.

Four-square Oilers obviously cannot end in a draw. Less obvious is the question which player has a winning strategy. And who has the winning strategy if the spoiler has the first move? (Answer on page 228)

11 · *Narratives*

Under this heading I have grouped together games in which the object is to produce words in some sort of narrative sequence rather than in isolation.

The first three – Telegrams, Alphabent and Constructapo – are more like competitions than games, in that each player works alone at the task and the winner is the one who produces the best, or funniest, or fastest, result. The others, two of them very old favourites which might have amused Victoria herself, are like sequential games, in which each player in turn adds a word or line to what has gone before. By no stretch of the imagination can these be described as 'competitive', but the enjoyment to be derived from them is too great to be missed on that account.

Telegrams

Any number of players
Adults and older children
Fun rather than competitive

Frequently described in the literature of word games is the one in which a random word is quoted and players are required to compose a telegram using its letters as initials of an appropriately phrased message. For instance, the word MESSAGE might produce:

MEET ETHEL STATION SATURDAY AND GET EARWIGS

or MY ELBOW STUCK: SEND A GREASED EGGCUP.

A little more spice may be added to the exercise by assuming that a given telegram consists merely of a name. Players then have to reconstruct the meaning by using the letters of the name acronymically. If the message can be related to the name, so much the better. Thus Napoleon might send a message that reads:

NEED ARMY. PREPARING OFFENSIVE. LEFT ELBA OTHER NIGHT.

The game is more amusing than competitive: I have never been able to discover who wins it, or why.

Alphabent

A small group of players
Mainly for adults
Amusing but isolationist

Alphabent is one of several games which I thought I invented, only to discover that the American National Puzzlers League had planted the flag there before me. Still, to give sour grapes their due, it is a very easy idea and I dare say has often been thought of before in the history of word games.

The basic idea is to write a sentence, paragraph, or even short story, consisting of 26 words beginning with successive letters of the alphabet. Hyphenated words may, but need not, count as one.

A prize-winning entry from the 1978 NPL Convention runs thus:

A brilliant Chinese doctor exhorted four graduating hospital interns: 'Just keep looking, men – no other prescription quickly relieves sore throats, unless veterinarians wilfully X-ray your zebras.'

The author of this alphabent is recorded only under the pseudonym Mona Lisa. The need to mind your Xs and Zs (not to mention Ps and Qs) before embarking on your ABCs no doubt accounts for the similarity between hers and one of my brother Graham's contributions to the genre, to wit:

A brilliant Cockney doctor emerged from Gynaecology, having incautiously just knocked long-suffering matron's neurologist out – protesting (quite rightly so) that untrained veterinarians wouldn't've X-rayed your zygoma.

My own first attempts at the alphabent need not be recorded. They pale to insignificance compared with the countless effusions of brother Graham, who immediately took to the art form like a duck to syrup of figs.

As birds can dive even from great heights, I just know larks must nest on pinnacles, quietly recollecting shattered thoughts, until violent winds xenomorphosize yon zones.

A bee, collecting dewy emanations from gladioli, homed in jerkily, knocking lumpy, misshapen nodes on particularly queer-looking roses, showering the underlying vegetation with xanthic (= yellow) zygospores.

A born coward, Darius eventually found great happiness in judicially kicking loud-mouthed nepotists openly picking quarrels, rightly saying that unkindness vitiated warring Xerxes' youthful zeal.

His masterpiece is surely the following 51-word poem, in which, having reached Z, he turns round and travels back to A. (I call it a poem for the sake of argument.)

A brilliant crystal, descending earthwards from
    glowering heavens,
introducing jewel-like, kaleidoscopic
luminescence, moved noiselessly over
    palatial quadrangles,
reflecting silent transformations under
    vaulted windows,
xanthisizing yellowing zones, yew-lined xysts,
winding vagrantly upwards toward
    sequestered rooftops –

quiescent posterns of neglected mansions,
lonely knolls, joyless, inhospitable houses –
gliding,
    falling ever downwards,
        cascading
            brightly
                away . . .

One way of playing Alphabent communally is by the passing-on method: each player in turn adds the next word to a specimen, passes it to his left, receives one from his right, and so on twenty-six times.

For a competitive game, the following method is quite workable. Three players in succession call out the A, B and C words, and the winner is the player who completes the alphabetical continuation either first or to best effect (as voted on by the others). For example:

Arnold After . . .
Byron buying . . .
Coleridge chocolate . . .

. . . and so on.

Alphabent can also be played orally for further amusement – see page 53.

Constructapo

Any number of players
Mainly for adults
A long, quiet, not very competitive game

My title for a well-known race game whose results can yield amusement out of all proportion to the simplicity of the idea. Players should come equipped with material to work on, or you may prepare it all yourself beforehand.

At each round, one player dictates a list of words in alphabetical order. The list will have been compiled by taking a stanza from a poem – the obscurer, the better – and pulling it apart. The winner is either the first player to produce a reasonable reconstruction of the stanza, complete with rhymes where appropriate, or, if preferred, the first to reproduce it exactly.

See what you can make of this one:

A	GONE	MY	SHOES
AND	HAS	MY	SINGING
AND	HEAR	MY	THE
ARE	I	OF	THE
BITS	IT'S	OVER	TO
FALLEN	LONG	ROAD	WAY
FOLK	MOUNTAIN	SAYING	WITS

You will find it reconstructed – properly – on page 228.

Consequences

Any number of players
Any age
Fun rather than competitive

I make no apology for including a game which is described as 'old-fashioned' even in the 1881 book of *In-Door Amusements and Fireside Fun* – and even though it is not really a game in the competitive sense of the word. It can still be fun to play, after all these years.

Each player is given a sheet of paper and starts by writing at the top an adjective or adjectival phrase descriptive of a male person – e.g. 'boring', 'happy-go-lucky', 'fast-talking', etc. The top of the paper is then folded over forwards so as to conceal it, and the paper passed to the player's left-hand neighbour.

On the second line of each sheet is then written the name of a male person, gentleman or bloke, whether real or fictitious. This, too, is concealed by folding over and passed to the right.

This procedure is followed ten times in all, the complete sequence of things to be written being as follows:

1. Adjective describing man
2. Man's name
3. Adjective describing woman
4. Woman's name
5. Place where they met
6. What he gave her
7. What he said to her
8. What she said to him
9. The consequence(s)
10. What the world said about it (or, as a concession to the march of progress, what the media said about it).

When all ten have been written, the sheets are passed round for the last time. Each player unfolds the one falling to their lot and reads it out loud (in turn, of course) with the addition of a few stock phrases here printed in italics. A final result might be:

1. Shy and retiring . . .
2. Erich von Thunderbold . . .
3. *met* the amazingly hirsute . . .
4. Pippa Poppaea . . .
5. in the back of a Mini.
6. *He gave her* a spoonful of Guinness
7. *and said:* 'Fancy a quick one?'
8. *She said to him:* 'Was that the telephone?'
9. *The consequence was* they entered themselves for the Derby . . .
10. *and the world said:* 'And that's how Mafeking was relieved.'

Headlines

Any number of players
Adults and older children
Fast and fun

I once devised a variation on Consequences to be played with a special pack of cards. It can be adapted for pencil and paper by playing as follows:

Each player writes a word or phrase at the top of a piece of paper, folds it over, and passes it to the left to be continued. Five entries and folds are made, the object being to compose a newspaper headline in the following format:

1. Personal description .
2. Type of person
3. Transitive verb in present tense
4. Object of verb
5. Place of occurrence.

Which, in case any doubt remains, may be clarified by examples of finished products when read out:

OUT-OF-WORK / VICAR / SEEKS / WHITE-
  COLLAR JOB / IN COAL-MINE
MYSTIFIED / FISHMONGER / DEMANDS /
  LOBOTOMY / UNDERNEATH THE ARCHES
HAPPY-GO-LUCKY / MOTHER OF SIX /
  BLAMES / COMMUNIST INFILTRATION /
  IN GRAVEYARD
HOUNDED / DOG TRAINER / PAYS FOR /
  VIOLA LESSONS / IN SWIMMING POOL
SELF-CONFESSED / PSYCHIATRIST / EATS /
  DIGITAL WATCH / ON TOP OF BIG BEN

Pass It On

Not too many players: best for four
Any age
Hilarious if played sensibly

My title for an age-old game which everybody knows and of which no example is needed – but you'll get one just the same.

It's the one where each player has a piece of lined paper, writes at the top the first line of a story with a few words spilled over on to the next line, folds it over so that only the over-spill is visible, passes it on to the player on his left, receives one from the player on his right, continues the line which has just been started . . .

But enough of this. With any luck the story you finish up with will sound nothing like the following. An oblique stroke indicates where the previous line ended:

Once upon a time there were three out-of-work bears,
each of whom / was loved in succession by Louis XV, a French king
famous for / about half an hour. Caesar, however, the gates of the camp
having been fortified / with a glass of tonic wine. Suddenly everyone wanted / to know if it was true that Goldilocks
was wearing / a décolleté mackintosh, when Madame de Pompadour
promptly started / up a four-horsepower chariot. The Gauls soon declared themselves / bankrupt and wondered how long it would be before / they returned from chopping trees in the woods.
'Oh,' said / the Queen, 'I hope I haven't interrupted anything.' To this,
Louis replied: / '5,000 javelins, 22 elephants & a packet of pins.'
But this / seems as good a place as any to boil my shoes
so I'll just / remind you of what Mamma Bear said. 'Young lady,'
she began, ' / I must say this is better than the game we played last week.'

You will soon discover that this was composed by four players, three of whom were concentrating on definite but unrelated themes (bears, courtesans and ancient Romans). Note how careful they have been to ensure that each over-spill leads into a sentence which holds together (except at the start of line four): this makes the nonsense stand out much better than it would if everything was completely haphazard. In this connection, note also that the over-spill of the last line ends with an open inverted comma, warning the next player that speech is expected. The result can be spoiled if it is not clear that the over-spill itself is part of someone's speech.

Another version of the game is based on the assumption that a broadcasting newsreader has got his notes in a muddle: the method of play is the same, but the newscasting background imposes a unity of style which makes the nonsense more effective. One such bulletin might begin:

> The Bolivian Minister of Nuts and Bolts
> has arrived / in spite of protest marches
> threatened by / workers in the treacle industry.
> Their purpose / is thought to be sabotage, but
> the Prime Minister / is unlikely to make a statement
> before / . . .

and so on.

An even better variant is that which purports to produce poetry, for want of a better name. The first player writes a line which establishes a rhythm and an opening rhyme, and passes it on without folding over. The second adds a line which rhymes with the first, and another which starts a second rhyme. He then folds the paper over so that only his last line is visible. This gives the next player a line to rhyme with, and so on, each in turn writing two lines, of which the first rhymes with the previous player's last, and only the second is left visible to the next person. Thus:

> I'll tell you an epic that never began:
> It started, I think, with the Siege of Sedan –
> There was a young lady who watched from afar
> But always from the comparative safety of her car; [Ugh!]
> It was, I repeat, a decrepit saloon
> Propelled by the gas from a hot-air balloon:
> She flew through the air with the greatest of ease
> And settled to rest on the points of her knees.
> It can't be described as a graceful descent

And tends to leave one of your handlebars bent.
But enough of this twaddle. The Siege of Sedan
Is thought to have ended before it began.

12 · *Cross Words*

Sir Anthony Dewlap Milord, with great respect, milord, a crossword puzzle is a form of puzzle, milord, in which a number of numbered squares in a chequered arrangement of – er – squares, milord, have to be filled in with letters, milord, these letters forming words, milord, which words are read both horizontally and vertically, milord – that is, both across and down, if your Lordship follows me – and which words may be deduced from certain descriptions or clues which are provided with the puzzle, milord, these descriptions having numbers, milord, and these numbers referring to the squares having the corresponding numbers, milord, which are to be filled in with the correct letters and words according to the descriptions which have the corresponding numbers, milord, whether horizontally or vertically, as the case may be. Does your Lordship follow me?

Mr Justice Snubb No.

Sir Anthony Dewlap Your lordship is too modest . . . Now as a rule, milord, the descriptions or clues provided are brief and the correct solutions are the names of mythical animals and Biblical characters, prepositions, foreign towns, classical writers, obscure musical instruments, vegetables, little-known adjectives, and so forth . . .

I quote this extract from the case of The Bishop of Bowl, Earl Rubble, Evadne Lady Smail, John Lickspittle, General Glue and others versus Albert Haddock – from, of course, A. P. Herbert's collection of *Misleading Cases* – for the simple reason that I could not possibly improve on the definition of a crossword. And it must be the only case on record of a claim of libel involving a crossword – in this case, one in which the solutions to the most scurrilous clues proved to be the names of the plaintiffs.

Lest it be thought to reflect upon the competence of judges, we might bear in mind that Herbert was writing only a few years after crossword puzzles were invented in the form in which we know them now. Even the main body of the *Oxford English Dictionary* has never heard of the crossword. Not surprisingly, it always comes as a surprise to people to learn that such puzzles date only from the nineteen-twenties.

(The crossing of words themselves, however, is of great antiquity. The earliest and best known example was found scratched on the surface of a Roman plough-stone:

S A T O R
A R E P O
T E N E T
O P E R A
R O T A S

It has variously been interpreted as a Christian symbol or merely as a clever sentence translatable as 'Arepo the sower holds the wheels with care.')

The games in this section all involve writing words in boxes and in such a way as to cross one another. Some of them might be described as competitive crosswords, in that players either compete to produce the best crossword on a given theme, or, better still, take turns to add words to the pattern. Others, such as that which I call Wordsworth but which is well known to millions of word-gamers under many different names, are less like the conventional crossword puzzle. But they all involve the crossing of words and form a highly distinctive group within the great family of written word games.

Double Cross

Two players
Any age
Quiet but competitive

The simplest way of playing a crossword game for two players is to start with a grid of from eight to fifteen squares each way.

The first player enters a word in the top left-hand corner – or anywhere else, if it comes to that – after which the two play alternately. At each turn they enter a word or phrase which properly fits in, crossword-fashion, with any word or phrase already entered. For each entry the player scores 1 point per letter entered. If you like, you can add a bonus of, say, 10 points for being the last to play. Or, for greater subtlety, exact a penalty of 10 points for being the last to enter a word. In the latter case you have the additional objective of always leaving an opportunity for your opponent to follow you, thus ensuring that the grid gets thoroughly filled up. Obviously, if one player tries to do his opponent down by claiming he cannot go, his opponent may force him to play by pointing out where he *can* go.

Alphacross or Alphabet Race

Two or more players
Adults and older children
Requires thought

Famed word-scrabbler Gyles Brandreth describes in one of his millions of books a game called Alphabet Race, whose title I have changed slightly because its original name could apply to several different games. Any number may play, but two is as good a number as any, if not better, and I will assume it to be operative in the following description.

The basic idea is very simple. Each player writes out a complete alphabet. The two then compile a crossword between them. Each player crosses off the letters of his own alphabet one at a time as he writes them in for the first time. The first to use all twenty-six letters wins. Notice that a letter must be written in before you cross it off. If you write AXES crossing with a previously written word EXIT you may not delete the X from your alphabet.

These rules are not complete on their own, and I have played the game in several different ways to find out which is

best. Suggestions follow, but you may vary them by agreement.

First of all, how large a crossword grid should you use? You
could just play it on squared paper and extend as far as you like
in all directions. The trouble with this is that eventually you
will discover a few long words like POLYTETRAFLUORO-
ETHYLENE which exhaust all 26 letters in a couple of turns.

If you are going to follow standard crossword patterning,
with blacked out squares between letters not belonging to the
same word, then you should start off with at least 11 × 11 (for
two players; if more players, more squares). This can be
reduced to 9 × 9 if you separate such letters by thickening the
lines between them rather than blacking out whole squares.
Alternatively, of course, you can play it like my game of Lynx
(page 143), using a printed crossword grid from a newspaper
or magazine.

It seems to me that there is a drawback to the simplest form
of Alphacross in that the first player has a great advantage.
With careful play between two equally matched contestants
the first to go should always get through all 26 letters first. You
should, therefore, play an even number of games, so that both
players have an equal number of first moves in the long run.

Another means to the same end is to ensure that both have
the same number of turns by allowing the player who went
second to have a final turn if and after the first player crosses
off his twenty-sixth letter. In this case I recommend that the
second player be held to win if he also crosses off his twenty-
sixth letter as a result.

As to scoring, if you want it, the simplest method is to count
1 point for each letter left in the loser's alphabet. For something more interesting you could ascribe values to letters, such
as A = 1, B = 2, . . . Z = 26, or in accordance with the letter
frequency table on page 223.

The strategy of play is obvious. Choose longer rather than
shorter words and those containing more rather than fewer
different letters. Concentrate first on getting rid of the
awkward letters J, Q, V, W, X, Z, or you may have difficulty

in fitting them in when the grid is fuller. Letter K is not so awkward: often it is best dealt with in combination with a preceding C at the end of a word or a following N at the beginning. Try to leave easy letters till last, especially in pairs or clusters that go together, such as NG, GH and so on. This doesn't mean, of course, that you should make a point of avoiding easy letters early on; most of them will naturally come out in the wash anyway.

I have let it go without saying (but I suppose I should just mention it) that each word entered in the grid must connect with at least one other word already there. I would also recommend a rule that no word may be repeated in the same game.

Scramble

Two to six players
Adults and older children
A long, quiet game

Although the title doesn't tell you what the game is about, it quite well describes the competitive panic which ensues as everyone tries to fill their squares up before everyone else. Scramble can be very nerve-racking if taken too seriously, so is best played in a mellow mood, perhaps as an after-dinner exercise. It too is from the collection of Gyles Brandreth.

Method of play Each player draws a grid of squares. A reasonable size is 10 × 10. If bigger, the game goes on too long; if smaller, there isn't enough room for variation. One player announces a theme, which should be a word small enough to fit the grid – let us say *transport*. Each player enters this word into his grid along the top row starting at the first space. They then have to complete a crossword, filling in unlettered squares as blanks where necessary, in such a way that all words and phrases entered are relevant to the stated theme. The game ends almost as soon as one player has filled his grid and calls 'Stop!', except that the others are allowed to finish the word they are writing. It is advisable to observe a rule that the 'stopper' must have filled at least half his squares with letters, i.e. fifty or more of a 10×10 grid, before he may end the game.

Scoring Each player passes his crossword to the person on his left to be marked, and marks that of his right-hand neighbour by examining the entries, and, if they are all acceptable, giving him a score consisting of 1 point for each letter written in. Mis-spellings and words of doubtful validity are dealt with as follows.

If an entry is mis-spelt, none of its letters may score; but no penalty is exacted for any of the words crossing it in the other direction unless they are mis-spelt or non-valid on their own account.

An entry may be considered doubtful if it is not a recognized phrase or is of only indirect relevance to the subject. For example, with the theme of transport one player essayed *pi* on the argument that it was an essential property of any wheel. Such questions must be put to the company, and I recommend the procedure that a word is valid if at least one opponent accepts it. (If only two play, they will have to fight it out between them!) If a word or phrase is not accepted, it is left unscored in the same way as if it were mis-spelt.

As a refinement, 10 points may be added to the stopper's score if he succeeded in filling more squares with letters than anyone else, and 10 points deducted if anyone else filled in more letters than the stopper.

Rules Certain rules should be agreed upon beforehand. For example:

1. Are proper names allowed, such as racing drivers or makes and models of car?
2. Are abbreviations allowed, such as *AA* or *RAC*?
3. May the same, or very nearly the same, word be entered more than once, such as *tram* and *trams*, or *alight* and *alighted*?
4. Are phrases allowed as well as single words, such as *on*

tow? If so, may they be split so that one constituent word appears in one part of the grid and the other(s) in another?

For myself, I am inclined to forbid abbreviations and duplications.

Hints The longer the words, the fewer the blanks, the higher the score. Short words are only economical of blanks if they interlink in large areas, but this is hard to achieve when you are racing against time. It is therefore not a bad idea to start by making the longest words you can – preferably of full row or column length – either around the outside of the grid or running vertically downwards from more or less alternate letters of the opening word. You are not obliged by law to

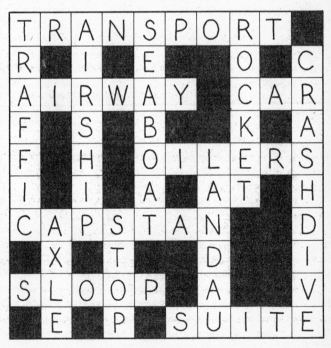

black out unlettered and unusable squares (only lettered squares will count towards the score), but it is advisable to do so as soon as you can establish which they are as this makes it easier to see what options remain open to you.

The Scramble crossword on the theme of transport (p. 135) scored 66. The word *suite* was accepted as being applicable to cabin cruisers and the like, but *at* ('a preposition much used in transport, as in "the train now standing *at* platform three"') incurred the deduction of two points.

Sinko

Two players
Adults and older children
Short, but challenging

A disconcerting feature of writing about games is that the best ones tend to be so short and apparently simple that there is little to say about them. Therefore those most worth playing take up little space and are easily missed. Sinko, a gem of a game, is one such. It seems to have been first described by Dave Silverman – a well-known puzzler – in the American magazine *Word Ways*. I did not see the original, and my account is taken from Ross Eckler's in *Games & Puzzles*, No. 62. Eckler, rather curiously, states that the last to add a word wins, but outlines a strategy for the second player which, if followed faithfully, guarantees him to lose! Either he has miscounted the moves or I have misunderstood his intention. No doubt you can work it out for yourself from the following description.

Play Draw a grid of 5 × 5 squares. Each plays in turn, and the last to be able to add a word to it wins. The first player enters any five-letter word into any one of the five horizontals or five verticals. The second also enters a five-letter word, either parallel to the first or crossing it in the opposite direction by means of a shared letter. Play continues as each adds a five-letter word in either direction. Wherever words cross one another they must, of course, have the same letter in common, but it is not necessary (and can be dangerous) to make adjacent letters combinable. Whoever writes in the last word wins. This may be because the grid is full up, or because the other player cannot add a word using the letter combinations available, or because he can see certain loss and resigns.

To illustrate the procedure, here is a game from actual play:

M	A	N	S	E
A			N	X
N	O	N	E	T
I	N	T	E	R
C	O	B	R	A

The order of word entry was: COBRA, EXTRA, MANIC, INTER, SNEER, NONET, MANSE. The fact that it contains seven complete words shows that the first player won, the second being unable to conjure up a word matching any of the patterns A..NX, A.ONO, N.NTB.

Notes In any game where the last to move wins it is interesting to work backwards from the final position to see if loss was inevitable. In the example above it is clear that NONET was a losing move for the second player, since the first won by entering MANSE. Did the second player then have a winning alternative?

I think he did, by entering MORSE in the top row. (It also means a walrus, in case anyone claims that the code of that name should be spelt with a capital.) Now the first player cannot fill either of the two remaining columns, since the second will win by filling the other. Two such words would be OUTDO and RHOMB. Similarly, since no English word has the pattern A..NX, only two rows can be filled; and the second player is bound to win, as it is a comparatively simple matter to find a horizontal word which would make all verticals impossible.

If MORSE wins for the second player, then SNEER was properly a losing move for the first on his previous turn. Could the first have made a winning word instead of SNEER in this position?

M				E
A				X
N				T
I	N	T	E	R
C	O	B	R	A

The answer to this depends to some extent on whether or not column two may be filled with AMINO. My nearest dictionary to hand recognizes this word only in the hyphenated compound *amino-acid*, so I will proceed on the assumption that it is not acceptable. In this case the first player can win by finding a horizontal word which will make all verticals impossible, and a safe bet would be MAIZE in the top row, leaving A..NO, I..TB and Z..ER – at least, I cannot find any reasonable continuation for these patterns offhand, and I'm not going to spend hours in the loo with my *Compact OED* over the problem. If now the second player writes NONET, the first wins with ADDAX (a type of antelope); or, if the second enters ADMIX, the first concludes with NIGHT. Or something along those lines.

If MAIZE wins, then INTER was a mistake for the second player on his second turn. Could he have done better?

Undoubtedly! BANJO in the second column kills off all four remaining horizontals by leaving as opening clusters MB-, AA-, NN- and IJ-. As there are two remaining verticals, the second player is bound to win.

We are left with the fascinating discovery that the first player lost the game on only his second move when he entered MANIC. This does not necessarily mean that EXTRA was a winning entry for the second player on his first turn, but it would be too time-consuming to backtrack any further. Perhaps you would like to see for yourself what happens if AMINO is an acceptable word. Of course, it is always easier to identify winning moves with the benefit of hindsight than to calculate them in advance *sur le champ*.

Generally, it is obvious that if the first five words entered all go in the same direction then the first player will win, since there is an odd number of them. The second player is therefore rarely wise to enter his first word in parallel with his opponent's opening, as it is often an easy enough matter for the first to find a third parallel word which kills off all five lines in the opposite direction. A critical position is always reached when the entry of a new word in one direction kills off all remaining in the other, and you should avoid making the killer word unless you can calculate a certain win from it.

In Ross Eckler's description of the game it is stated that the second player usually seems to have the advantage. I found this to be so when I played around with the game in the abstract, i.e. against myself, but in real play I have recorded more wins by the first than by the second player. A game of several rounds can be created, with some additional interest, by decreeing that the winner is the first player to win in *both* positions, i.e. as first and second player.

Another variant of possible interest (though I haven't tried it yet) is to permit up to two diagonal words, one from top left to bottom right, the other from top right to bottom left. Yet more complexity can be introduced – if that's your idea of fun – by permitting words to read in either direction!

Wordsworth or Crossword, Scorewords, Wordsquares, etc.

Two to six players, ideal for three
Adults and older children
A game of skill

This classic game is probably the simplest, best and most popular of them all. I don't know how old it is, but it can't be all that young. It is remarkably similar to Poker Patience or Poker Squares, a card game that became a fad on both sides of the Atlantic in the early part of the twentieth century – and I mean B.C. (Before Crosswords).

It's the game where you each draw a grid of squares and fill them up with letters called out by everybody in turn. Whoever makes the most and longest words gets the highest score and wins. It will come as no surprise to learn that no two groups seem to follow exactly the same rules: you may vary the number of squares in the grid, the extent to which words may overlap and the scores awarded for their length. I will therefore start with the plainest version of the game I have encountered, then describe the form I play myself. That should give you plenty of scope for developing your own variations.

Plain version If there are not more than four players, each one draws a grid of 5 × 5 squares on their paper. (Five should play on a 6 × 6 grid and six on a 7 × 7, but I will assume 5 × 5 in the following account.) After drawing the grid, make sure no one else can see what you are writing on your paper, otherwise you will probably lose.

Each player in turn calls out a letter of the alphabet. Everybody including the caller must write that letter in any vacant square of their own grid. The object is to put it in the most suitable position for forming a word or words in conjunction with whatever letters are called subsequently. Make certain that no new letter is called until everyone assures the caller, on their honour, that they have entered the previous one.

This continues until everyone has had the same number of

calls and all the squares are filled with letters except one. Each player completes his grid by filling the last square with any letter he likes.

Each player then works out his score. Scores are made only for words of three or more letters in consecutive squares of any row or column (not diagonal). Only one word may be scored in each row or column, and the scores are 3 for a word of three letters, 4 for one of four and 5 for one of five. As there are five rows and five columns the highest possible score is 50.

Even in this plain version some players allow a minimal degree of overlap, namely: If the first three and the last three letters of a row or column form words, both may be scored. Thus a line consisting of LOGEM may score 3 each for LOG and GEM. In this case, of course, the highest possible score is 60. And if you allow diagonals as well (not really recommended) then the maximum is 72.

If you use a grid larger than 5×5 then you need some form of jumped-up scoring to give significantly larger scores for longer words – say, for example, three letters 1, four letters 3, five 5, six 7, seven 10.

Multiple overlap version In my circle we play with as many overlaps as can be made, *provided that no word is contained entirely within another*. A word of five letters scores 10, so the highest possible total is 100. Here are some examples of line scores with permitted overlaps:

AKSET   scores 3 (for SET)
APSEB   scores 4 (for APSE)
APEGT   scores 6 (for APE and PEG)
AGEGG   scores 6 (for AGE and EGG)
APSET   scores 7 (for APSE and SET)
APEST   scores 8 (for APES and PEST)
APEGG   scores 9 (for APE, PEG and EGG)
ASSET   scores 10 (for ASSET)

Note that the score of 10 for a five-letter word is enough to make overlaps unnecessary: ASSET is worth more than ASS plus SET. Note also that in the sixth line you could not also score 3 for APE since it is entirely contained within the word APES for 4.

What constitutes a good score depends on the number of players. If there are only two of you then you fill 13 of the 25 squares by your own choice, enabling you to make at least three five-letter words for 30 points minimum. Skilful use of the other 12 should enable you to at least double that score.

Advice on play The most obvious verbal skill required is that of knowing a good stock of short words, especially those involving awkward letters. It is also handy to know whether a given letter is likely to be more useful early in a word, and therefore be best placed near the top or the left of the grid, or more towards the end, calling for a bottom or right-hand entry. The tables on page 224 may be interesting in this respect.

By the time you have five or six letters in, you will be looking for useful digrams rather than early or later positions, for example BL, BR, CH, CL, CR (early) or CT (late), FL, FR, GH (final), GL, GR, PL, PR, RT (late), SC, SH, SL, SP, ST, TH, WH.

With about half the grid filled you may already have a five-letter word and will have ideas about the best use of most rows or columns. It can be useful to keep one line available as a 'rubbish dump' for letters that will not combine with the skeletal words you already have, but there is a danger of over-using this device: filling it up early is a sign that you are not making the best of your opportunities.

Stronger players of this game can take great advantage of weaker by planning word patterns involving awkward letters, such as K and V, then calling the awkward letters and relying on the weaker players to come up with the necessary Es and Ss and so on. This is the point at which gamesmanship takes over from verbal mastery. A sensitive player can often tell which word one or more opponents are trying to make, so that he can either cash in on it himself or throw in the J-Q-X-Z monkey-wrench to make it impossible.

Since everyone needs vowels, everyone tends to leave it to everyone else to nominate them. It is amazing how long it may take for anyone to break down and call E or A; sometimes E may not be called at all. This makes it all the more important to combine your consonants well. As a matter of policy it is usually best to call the most obscure letter of all the ones that will actually enable you to form a word in your own grid, if only one of three letters.

If you play the overlapping version, don't let yourself be mesmerized by the score of 10 for a five-letter word. It isn't worth getting your statutory two fivers (in a three- or four-player game) if your other 16 squares are filled with rubbish. Remember three threes is almost as good as one five.

Lynx

Two players, versions for three or four
Mainly for adults
A lengthy but rewarding game

Doing yesterday's crossword is like reading yesterday's news. You may not have seen the solution, but the fact that it has been published takes all the bite out of it. I devised this game to enable my wife and self to fill up yesterday's undone crossword pattern with some sense of competition and achievement. As such it works quite well for two, the number assumed to be playing in the account below. Modifications are suggested for three or four players at the end of the main description.

For each game – which shouldn't take more than half an hour – you need a printed crossword pattern from a newspaper or magazine. (You don't need the clues.) You could draw your own pattern if you prefer, but it is much more convenient to take one ready made.

Method of play Each plays in turn by entering a word into the grid in such a way as to fit one light exactly and to link properly with any other words that cross it. Each such entry earns a score based on the length of the word and the number of links it contains (whence the title). Any word, name or phrase is permitted which one would normally expect to find in a published crossword, but it is not permitted to split phrases between different lights. (Example: For the phrase *take cover* you could not in one turn enter *take* in one light and *cover* in a different one, but you could enter both words in a light of nine spaces.)

The first word must be written in one of the shortest lights in the pattern; e.g. if the pattern contains no light shorter than four spaces (as in the paper I take), then the first word must go in any one of the four-space lights. The score for this entry is 1 point per letter.

Thereafter, each new word must link with at least one other existing word in the pattern. The score made for it is 'length times links': that is, the number of letters in the word or phrase entered *multiplied by* the number of links it makes with previously entered words. A link, of course, is a letter which is already there when you start to write.

Example: For entering the word BALANCE into a light consisting of . . L . . . . you would score length 7 times links 1 = 7. For entering it in a light containing the three links . A . A . C . you would score length 7 times links 3 = 21. And so on. Keep a running total for each player as the game progresses.

Play continues alternately until one player declares that he cannot think of anything to enter. If his opponent also cannot play further, then the declarer adds a bonus of 10 points to his final total. If he can, however, he may continue playing and scoring for as long as he is able; but he does not get a bonus when he finishes, and declarer may not make any more entries even if he thinks of a continuation.

Irregularities It is advisable to announce what you propose to enter before entering it, in case of disputes as to spelling or acceptability. No hard and fast rules can be given to cover acceptability: regular crossword solvers know what sort of words and (particularly) phrases are acceptable. I am inclined to suggest that anything is acceptable which can be shown in print within five minutes of making the claim.

There are two ways of dealing with the circumstance of one player's making an entry which turns out to be mis-spelt or not to fit the light properly. If you are writing in pencil, erase the entry and miss that turn. If in ink, let it stand but score nothing for it. If the word is too short for the light, repeat the last letter as often as necessary; if too long, omit as many of the final letters as necessary.

Three players Because Lynx is basically a two-player game, in which each move is made with a view to complicating the next (opponent's) one but favouring the one after (your own), the only satisfactory way of adapting it for three is to adopt a 'split partnership' score as follows. Play continues until all three pass in succession – there is no finishing bonus, but a player who has once passed must drop out. Assuming that play was made in a clockwise direction – passing regularly to the left – each player finishes by doubling his own score and adding to it the (undoubled) score of the player on his right.

Four players Four is a more convenient number than three, as the participants can play in partnerships of two each. Partners sit opposite each other and play alternately, with a single partnership score being kept between them. Consultation is not permitted between partners, since the stronger player will dominate the play and the game will effectively finish as a contest between only two players.

An amusing variant, however, is to follow the rule that the person whose turn it is to write an entry must do so in a light designated by his partner. In other words, one player thinks of his best possible continuation and tells his partner *where* it is but not *what* it is. If that partner cannot fill the required light, it remains empty and the turn passes to the left. If the following player – an opponent – can fill the designated light, he may do so and then also take his proper turn in a light designated by his partner. I recommend this version. It may sound vicious, but it requires each player to know his partner's verbal strengths and weaknesses and so makes the idea of partnership an essential rather than an incidental feature of the game.

Pi

Two players
Mainly for adults
Fast but thought-provoking

Why Pi?

Why not? Presumably there is a good reason for it, but for that you would have to ask the inventor, John Shepherd, who first introduced it in the monthly letter of a group of postal gamesters called the Knights of the Square Table.

Pi is the simple end of a scale whose other extreme is represented by the game of Black Squares. I hope I describe it accurately: my source is Ross Eckler in *Games & Puzzles*, whose highly condensed account is hard to follow.

It is played on a squared grid with a minimum recommended size of $5 \times 5 = 25$ squares. Each player in turn writes a letter of the alphabet in any square, or else challenges the previous player's letter. The loser is the first player unable to move without breaking a rule, or to fail to defend himself against a challenge.

The rules are:

1. In each row and column, three or more consecutive letters must form a word when read in the appropriate direction (left to right or top to bottom).
2. A letter may not be entered which makes it impossible to complete a word of two or more letters by subsequent additions in the same row or column.

You may, therefore, challenge your opponent for failing to make a word under rule 1; he loses immediately if he cannot prove the existence of the word by reference to the dictionary, but you lose immediately if he can. Similarly, he can only meet a challenge under rule 2 by showing how the letter he has just added can be incorporated into a word of two or more letters. A challenge could also be used in a process of bluff. Conceivably, you may make an entry which breaks a rule, then challenge your opponent if he adds another letter instead of challenging you. The onus is then on him to make sense of your bluffed entry.

Black Squares

Two players
Mainly for adults
A long and deep game

Harry Woollerton, the inventor of this and many other 'Games You Haven't Played Before' (the title of his series in *Games & Puzzles* magazine), claims Black Squares to be to ordinary crossword games as Chess is to Chinese Checkers. I'll go along with that, speaking as an ex-Chess-player who gave it up because life seemed too short. Black Squares requires more mental calculation than ever appears on paper, and an outside observer might be forgiven for thinking the players have actually gone to sleep between moves. If you're intending to play it at speed, without proper thought, allow about two hours. It really is the game for word-gaming experts.

Before embarking upon its description I must confess to having messed about with it to some extent. This is partly because Mr Woollerton's original rules seem incomplete to me: I had difficulty in working out the order of events, and uncertain situations arose which they did not appear to cover. Further, the rule permitting any number of letters to be entered anywhere in the grid on any one turn (provided that they fit the crossword) struck me as rather too lax, and in this and one or two other small respects I have deliberately tightened up the discipline of play. If there is too much choice it takes too long to make a decision, and I have cut some of the choice down in order to get the game going at least a little faster.

To start Black Squares is played on a squared grid of any suitable size. The individual squares should be at least 1 cm each way and they should be inked or printed, not drawn in pencil. (This is because the game may involve substantial erasures.) A grid of 11 × 11 squares is sufficient for a 'quickie' game of about two hours.

General idea Black Squares is a crossword game to the extent that all the letters eventually entered into it must properly link with adjacent letters to form words in both directions. No part of the finished crossword may be entirely cut off from the rest of it. It is for the players to decide whether proper names and multi-word phrases are allowed, but I recommend sticking to basic rules: single words only, no names, not acceptable if not in the dictionary nearest to hand when challenged. Unusually, however, it is not the main aim of the game to make words. You gain nothing by doing so. Instead, the object is to score for identifying 'black squares', or for proving that a square claimed as black by your opponent can in fact be filled with a letter.

A black square, you will gather, is one which is incapable of being filled with a letter forming part of a genuine crossword. For example, if the word *grumpy* were entered in the grid, it would be possible to claim a black square immediately before the G and another immediately after the Y, since the word cannot be extended in either direction. But you couldn't claim a black square immediately before or after SET, which may be extended forwards into UPSET, RUSSET, etc., rearwards into SETTER, SETTLE, etc. or both ways at once into COSSETTING. Hence it is usually unsafe to complete an unextendable word such as *grumpy*, unless one end of it occurs at the edge of the crossword grid (you cannot claim black squares outside it!) or against an existing black square.

The need for both pen and pencil is explained as follows. When you enter letters or claim black squares you do so in pencil and it is then your opponent's turn. If he can successfully challenge them they are erased. If he accepts them as correct he inks them in. Thus you always start your turn by challenging or inking in, and end it by pencilling in. In the following description I am going to refer to inked-in letters as *black* and to pencilled in letters as *grey*. Only grey letters can be challenged.

Play The first player enters any letter in the centre square. Thereafter, each in turn must either (a) challenge the previous move or (b) ink it in and then either (1) claim one or more black squares or (2) pencil in one or more grey letters. These are explained in more detail below in the order in which they are most likely to occur in play. Note, however, that in the normal course of events you cannot both enter new letters and claim black squares in the same turn. Your first object is therefore to avoid giving your opponent any possible black squares.

Entering letters When you pencil letters into the grid they may extend an existing word, form a complete word or form a sequence that may be turned into a word. You may enter any number of letters, and they may be entered anywhere in the grid, provided always that each grey letter is in line with a black letter, or with a grey letter which in turn lines up with a black one, and also that any two adjacent letters are capable of being formed into a word.

Challenging grey letters You may challenge letters just pencilled in by your opponent on either of two grounds: that the word they make is mis-spelt or otherwise non-valid, or that they cannot possibly be incorporated into properly connected words.

Mis-spelt or non-valid words are settled by reference to the dictionary. As to allegedly non-connectable words, the challenged player may seek to justify them by pencilling in all the challenged connections necessary to prove that they will fit. Letter sequences which do not yet form words are not to be filled in unless specifically challenged.

If the challenge is successful, the grey letters are erased and the challenged player must enter different grey letters. There is no penalty, except that the challenged player is then obliged to enter letters: he may not claim black squares instead.

If letters are challenged for non-connectability, and the challenged player can in fact connect them by filling in all the necessary connections, then he may continue play himself by inking them in and claiming any black squares they may give rise to. Similarly, if his challenged words are validated by the dictionary, he may ink them in and claim black squares.

Claiming black squares To claim a black square, pencil a diagonal line through it. You may claim more than one black square in one turn, but may not enter letters in the same turn.

Challenging black squares If you accept as correct your opponent's claim of a black square, ink it in. For this, he scores 1 point.

To challenge a black square, pencil in a letter and make all the connections demanded by your opponent to show that it fits into the crossword. If these are accepted, ink them in, score 1 point for each disproved black square, and continue by claiming black squares or entering letters.

As I remarked earlier, this version of the game is not exactly as its inventor described; but it is the form I play and I can at least guarantee that it works. As witness:

Sample game The first eight moves of a game between Dickens and Eliot are illustrated on pp. 151–2. Dickens starts with an H in the middle and Eliot answers with the letters in frame 2. She might have in mind something like SHROVE or THROVE horizontally and CURVE(D) or SCARVES vertically: there is no shortage of possibilities.

In frame 3 Dickens has evidently seen such words and is content to go along with them. He has seen an alternative to SHROVE which also has S before H. The addition of P is interesting: there are not many words ending in either V (horizontally) or PO (vertically), so he may be thinking of a vowel in the common square following each of those endings. The U cuts out CARVE or SCARVES, suggesting rather CURVE or a derivative thereof.

Eliot, in 4, can see a nice alternative to CURVE but cannot see any to SHROVE horizontally. She therefore uses her turn to claim two black squares, one at each end of the envisaged word.

Dickens, however, has this sequence well covered, as his insertion of MUSHROOMS in frame 5 indicates. This gives him a safe black square claim, since the word surely cannot be

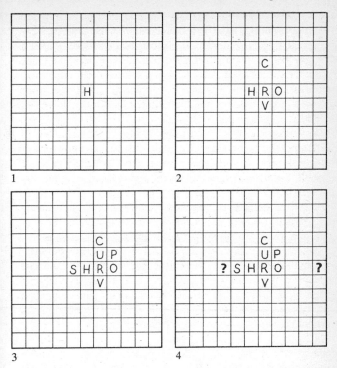

1 2 3 4

extended from the front. He scores 2 for filling in Eliot's
queried squares and is now into his proper turn. He could add
more letters but instead falls into Eliot's trap by querying the
square before CURV-. His opponent grants the black square
by filling it in, but . . .

Frame 6 shows that Eliot had thought of scurvy, giving her
2 points and some black square claims: one at each end of that
word, and another in the space involving PO and V discussed
above.

In 7, Dickens scores a packet. Accepting Eliot's squares on
either side of scurvy, he places I in the disputed square
(scoring a point) and adds spoil and vile to show how it fits in.

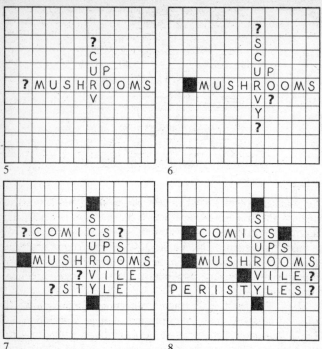

5

6

7

8

At this stage certain letter combinations are unaccounted for, namely CS caused by the S of SPOIL, OL and ME created by the conjunction of VILE and MUSHROOMS, and YL by the last letters of SCURVY and SPOIL. He is not obliged to justify these combinations by turning them all into words except where challenged to do so. But, for the sake of argument, let us assume that Eliot does so challenge him. In this case he completes all possible words as shown in the same frame (UPS, of course, is both a verb and a plural), leaving no odd letter combinations unaccounted for. He scores nothing for these. Now he is at the end of his challenges and into his proper turn. Obviously he will not add any further non-extendable words, otherwise Eliot will claim the appropriate black squares. But

9

he may complete his own turn by claiming black squares against the non-extendable words he has just created and accordingly does so as shown by the query marks in frame 7.

In the last frame shown on page 152, Eliot accepts and fills in three of the four claimed, but herself scores a point and a safe black square claim for thinking of PERISTYLES (an architectural term).

Hints The position in frame 7 illustrates a situation which often occurs but may be confusing at first. Consider UPS. Let us assume that it cannot be extended further forward than by one letter, to CUPS or TUPS or SUPS as the case may be. (I cannot think offhand of any longer words that would fit.) Since UPS is a word, it follows that either the square immediately in front of it is black or the square before that is black (i.e. before CUPS, etc.). The fact that *one* of them must be black does not, however, at this stage enable *either* of them to be claimed. Thus if Eliot queries the square before UPS, Dickens enters (say) CUPS across and RICH down, and queries the square before C. Or, if she queries the other one, Dickens fills it with (let us say) E to make COMES downwards, and then successfully claims as black the square between that E and UPS. It is not until more letters have been entered affecting these squares that either of them may successfully be claimed. At any stage during a game there may be several such ambiguous couplets, and both players must keep them very much in mind in order to spot when either of them can be used.

The end of the game is shown in frame 9, where it will be noticed that not all squares have been filled. This frequently happens when it becomes apparent to both players that no black squares can be claimed in a given area. For example, the top left corner can be filled with COSTAL, bottom left with COAL and ART, bottom right with INDEED and AGO horizontally, NO, EN (or EM) and ODE vertically, and top right with BOA horizontally (making BUS, OAST, AN) and EMS vertically. Usually it is the obvious words which remain unwritten while the obscure ones are entered as the result of challenges. In this game mention might be made of the animals PACA and URIAL; FARO is a card game, DUAN a division of a poem and TE the sharpened form of TI in the tonic sol-fa. (The tonic sol-fa is a boon to word-gamers, though many are not aware of the fact that it includes a whole series of modified forms for sharps and flats – see, for details, entry in even the smallest *(Concise) Oxford Dictionary of Music.*)

Sometimes a game can end without all squares being filled in and with one or more black squares known to be possible. This particularly occurs whenever the only remaining spaces include 'ambiguous couplets' of squares as described earlier. Neither player may wish to take his turn because he will inevitably give the other a black square. To cover this eventuality it is recommended that either player on his turn to play be permitted to pass. This does not prevent him from playing again should his opponent agree to take the next turn, but if his opponent passes as well then the game is at an end.

Yet another awkward situation can arise between careless players, for which no rule seems adequate. Theoretically there is nothing to stop the following sequence of events: Dickens writes in some letters; Eliot looks at them superficially, assumes they can be made into words, and accordingly inks them in. Then Dickens challenges Eliot to connect them, and neither is able to. Unless you agree to white them out there is nothing you can do to overcome this inelegant situation.

Therefore, to make the game workable, you must only write in letters which you honestly believe you can connect if challenged. Similar problems arise if unconnected letters are not challenged and it later transpires that they spoil the crossword. In this case it will merely have to be agreed to accept accidental non-words. It should go without saying that if a mis-spelling is accepted by the opponent, and inked in, then it must stand. Retrospective corrections are not allowed.

The skill required by Black Squares is only partly verbal. Memory has an important part to play, since you must carry in mind several alternative ways of filling a given area and keep track of the 'ambiguous couplets' described earlier. Also involved is some sort of positional thinking comparable with that demanded by abstract board games. At its simplest this is to be found in certain positions where it is only necessary to count the sequence of moves ('I go here, he goes there, me here, him there, me here, he claims black square') to discover whether or not it is safe to venture into a particular area of the board.

There are two obvious verbal tactics to employ. One is to adumbrate the 'ghost' of a word by entering letters that appear difficult to connect, such as S-Y-H (for SCYTHE), hoping that your opponent will fail to spot the connection and claim black squares. This ploy, however, is not easy to disguise: he may not spot the word you have in mind but will assume there is one and wait until you fill it in. A more cunning version of the device is to enter a ghost which you can see no way of connecting, but with sufficient confidence to suggest that you have a magnificent word up your sleeve. Your opponent accepts it, then on your turn you claim the black square(s) which he should have claimed himself. In adopting this bluff, however, you must be careful not to force 'impossible words' in related parts of the crossword.

A more effective tactic is to lay ghosts which are not too difficult to embody into subsequent words in positions such as create what may appear to be accidental letter sequences or juxtapositions in related areas. Of course, you will have worked out the connections in advance.

At the start of each turn, examine every part of the board for potential black squares. It often happens that a possibility remains overlooked for several moves after it has been created.

All in all, I think Black Squares is about the most intellectual word game ever invented, and I write about it with considerable admiration, not to say enthusiasm. It is, however, an acquired taste, and I must confess that I have not yet found an opponent willing to play it a second time round!

Ragaman

Two to six players, but the fewer the better
Mainly for adults
Games of competitive concentration

That great minds think alike is illustrated by the two closely related games described below. Ragaman, an evident anagram of anagram, was invented by Richard Sharp (GB) and first published in his *Best Games People Play*. Last Word, so called because his friends thought it the last word in word games (we are not told what his enemies thought), is the invention of Sid Sackson (US) and is detailed in his *Gamut of Games*. Both involve basically the same mechanics, though the dressing up is slightly different and there is considerable variation in the scoring systems. You may like to play both and then either decide which you prefer or else combine the two in some way. I rather favour the format of Ragaman with the scoring of Last Word.

My remark that fewer players make for a better game is based solely on the consideration that much thinking time tends to be taken, which is boring for those awaiting their turn.

The game is played on an odd-numbered squared grid: 5 × 5 is suitable for two players having a tea-break; 9 × 9 will do for six players serving a life sentence.

The first player starts by writing any vowel in the centre

square. Thereafter, each player in turn writes any letter anywhere in the grid, provided that it is adjacent to at least one other existing letter, whether horizontally, vertically or diagonally.

Having entered your letter, you now score the combined length of any word or words you can make which use that letter together with any horizontal, vertical or diagonal line of letters lying consecutively with it. Only one word may be made in any one direction (you will choose the longest, of course), giving a maximum of four possible words (remember that there are two diagonals). All the letters of a claimed word must lie consecutively, but they need not be in order. What you are actually making, more often than not, is not words but anagrams of words.

This will no doubt become clear by means of an illustration. The two squares shown represent the same two-player game, the first as it appeared half way through, the second as completed.

In the half-way-through diagram the numbers apply to squares in which the next player could add a letter by the rules of the game, and show the maximum score he could expect for doing so. For example, a letter in the top left corner could earn 3 in conjunction with AT, 2 in conjunction with U, and 3 with the diagonal MY – if, that is, a suitable letter can be found,

8	T$_7$	A$_9$	11	6
U$_8$	M$_2$	E$_4$	T$_{11}$	N$_{12}$
11	A$_3$	Y$_1$	W$_6$	9
8	H$_{10}$	E$_5$	9	4
6	S$_{13}$	9	4	

A$_{24}$	T	A	O$_{16}$	M$_{21}$
U	M	E	T	N
S$_{14}$	A	Y	W	O$_{20}$
N$_{15}$	H	E	S$_{18}$	A$_{23}$
O$_{17}$	S	Y$_{22}$	R$_{19}$	R$_{25}$

which I doubt. This diagram shows that at any given turn there are always one or more potentially best squares – the ones giving the highest possible scores – and of course it is an elementary point of strategy to try for the best theoretical scores first and gradually work down to the best you can get in practice. (At a more advanced strategic level you will also consider what potential score you are leaving to the next player, and may find it more profitable in the long run to compensate for a lower score by a safer position.)

The first player opened with the vowel Y in the middle; the second scored 2 for MY and the first then gained 4 for the A above the M, making AM and AY. The figures in the diagram show the order in which the twenty-five letters were placed, from which you can deduce who played what. The words made, and their scores, were as follows:

1st player	*2nd player*
(1) Y	(2) MY = 2
(3) AM, AY = 4	(4) YE, AE, ME = 6
(5) EYE, EA = 5	(6) WE, WE, WAY = 7
(7) WET, MAT = 6	(8) EMU, EAU, UT = 8

(There was some argument about EAU: I don't think I would have allowed it.)

| (9) YEA, AM, AT = 7 | (10) MATH, HE = 6 |

(MATH was rejected as an abbreviation of MATHEMATICS, which by British players is shortened to MATHS, but was accepted as a dialectical word meaning 'a mowing'. This opens the floodgates to several ensuing dialectical and Scottish words on which I will not comment further.)

(11) MUTE, THY, AT = 9
(12) UNMET, NEW = 8
(13) MATHS, SEWN = 9
(14) SH, US, YAWS = 8
(15) HEN, NAE, SUN = 9
(16) OAT, NO, TOW, OE = 10
(17) ONUS, SO, HOY = 9
(18) SWOT, HENS = 8
(19) WORST, ARE = 8
(20) ON, OAT, SO, OW = 9
(21) MOAT, MOTHY = 9
(22) ROSY, SOY, SHY, YE = 12
(23) MOAN, ASHEN, AWE = 12
(24) ANUS, AT, YAMS = 10
(25) MANOR, SORRY = 10

Had I been the first player, I might have claimed NOM at move 21 in return for accepting EAU at move 8, and, having earlier got away with NAE, might have put up a case for TWAE at move 23. Be that as it may, the first player wins by 97 to 94.

In case, like me, you dislike games involving lots of little scores with a tendency to very small margins of victory (which is one of the things I've got against Cribbage), you may prefer to follow Richard Sharp's suggested 'advanced' version, in which you may score for as many different words as you can make in any direction. Or you may give credit for longer words by boosting scores as follows: 2 letters = 2, 3 letters = 6, 4 letters = 10, 5 letters = 15, in which case the first player wins by 227 to 190. Or you may use Sid Sackson's system for Last Word, which is designed to give maximum credit for making words in as many different directions as possible. In this case the second player emerges as the winner, with 259 to 235 points.

Last Word

Two or more players
Mainly for adults
Another game of competitive concentration

The mechanics of Sid Sackson's game are essentially the same as for Ragaman. They are, however, if I may mix my metaphors, poured into a rather different mould.

Last Word requires a larger grid of 11 × 11, or even 13 × 13. To start off, the nine central squares are filled with letters at random, such as by opening a book at random and taking the first nine letters at the top of the page. For example, if the page began: 'Last Word requires . . .' then the central box of squares would be filled like this:

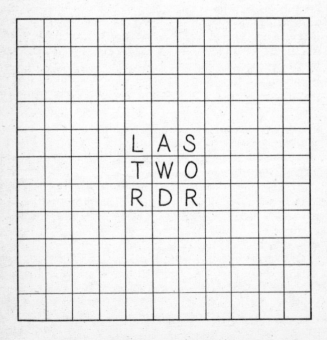

Play continues as in Ragaman: each player in turn adds a letter to any square adjacent to one containing a letter and claims the longest anagrammized word that can be made in any direction from it, using only consecutive lines of letters.

Your score is found by taking the lengths of all the words you can make and multiplying them together. For example, under this system the last two turns of the game illustrated for Ragaman would have scored as follows:

ANUS, YAMS, AT = 4 × 4 × 2 = 32
MANOR, SORRY = 5 × 5 = 25

In addition to the more sophisticated scoring, there is a nice touch to the way it finishes. It is not necessary to fill all the squares of the grid. Instead, the game ends as soon as a letter has been placed in at least one square along each of the four edges of the layout (for which purpose, presumably, a letter in a corner counts as reaching two edges). Thus a player in the lead can try to end the game sooner by going off in all directions, while those who are trailing can seek to hold him back by encouraging the growth of a central cluster. Their task is encouraged by a special rule of play which states that a player may not add a letter unless he can make words in at least two directions with it.

13 · *Fictionaries*

The first and original game in this section – the lexicographers' busman's holiday – has always been known to me simply as The Dictionary Game, though it forms the basis of a TV panel game known to millions as Call My Bluff. Richard Sharp, renewing the currency of a word unknown to Chambers but recorded in the *OED*, calls it Fictionary Dictionary, which seems to fulfil all the requirements of efficient nomenclature except possibly ease-of-saying-quickly-when-drunk. The basic gaming idea (or 'ludeme', to use a justly neglected technical term) can be extended to all sorts of other areas which have nothing to do with the dictionary as such and give rise to a number of variations which I will take pleasure in detailing throughout this chapter.

The idea is that an obscure word or phrase is presented to the players, who are required to write a suitable definition for it. These are then read out and voted upon without revealing who wrote what. Sources are identified after the vote, and your object is to spot the true definition while misleading everyone else into thinking your own definition is the correct one.

(In the TV programme, which serious word-gamers generally abhor, the various predetermined definitions are performed by members of Equity, each team having to guess which member of the other is telling the truth. The entertainment value of 'Call My Bluff' therefore lies in the performance rather than in the cleverness of the definitions themselves.)

As befits all popular games transmitted by word of mouth there are no universally agreed rules of play or scoring. The ones presented here are merely those that happened to evolve naturally within my circle of players. Feel free to change them and invent your own when you have got into the swing of things.

Fictionary Dictionary

Four to six players (best)
Mainly for adults
A lengthy but stimulating amusement

Let's describe the simplest way of playing it and add the provisos and embellishments later.

Players should dispose themselves in such a way as to prevent one another from seeing what they are writing. One player takes the dictionary, finds an obscure word whose true definition is suitably baffling or amusing, and announces the word and its spelling but not, of course, its meaning.

Each player then composes a dictionary-style definition intended to mislead opponents into thinking it the true one. This is written on a card or slip of paper and passed to the dictionary-holder. The dictionary-holder, meanwhile, writes out the true definition on his own slip.

When all are ready, the dictionary-master reads out the definitions one by one, slowly and clearly. If requested, he may read any or all of them a second or third time.

Starting with the player on his left and going in strict rotation, he calls upon each player to vote for the 'true' definition. (He himself has no vote, of course.)

Finally, he states the true definition and identifies who wrote what and who voted unwittingly for whom. Each player scores 1 point for selecting the true definition, plus 1 point for each opponent who voted for his own. The dictionary-keeper only scores if no one guessed the true definition, his score being 1 point per opponent – i.e. one less than the number of players.

The dictionary then passes to the left for the next round of play.

Optional rules and conventions Because the dictionary-keeper's score operates on a different basis, it is desirable for everyone to have the same number of turns at choosing the word to be defined. If not, the dictionary-keeper should score a flat 1 point if no one guesses the correct definition.

Time spent in word-searching can be cut by planning the game beforehand and ensuring that everyone comes to the party equipped with a stock of words for definition. In our circle we allocate each player a section of the dictionary to which his word-hunting must be restricted.

Depending on how you play, it may be desirable to ensure that everyone uses the same dictionary. Much of the skill of the game then lies in reproducing or spotting the style of the dictionary in the definitions quoted. This assumes that the dictionary-holder must write down the true definition word for word (though of course it is only necessary to give the first or major definition where there is a whole string of them). I mention this point only because there are players who prefer that the dictionary-holder rewrite the true definition in his own words, in which case the fun and skill lie in spotting one another's style of writing rather than in attuning oneself to that of the dictionary.

A convention followed in our circle is that the dictionary-holder should arrange his slips in strict alphabetical order of first word(s) of definition, so that there can be no possible bias in the order in which they are read out. Incidentally, he should read each slip as soon as it is passed to him to ensure that every word is legible and understandable; otherwise he may stumble or frown over an awkward word or phrase and give the game away. No harm is done by immediately passing the slip back with a query for correction before time is up.

As to how much time should be allowed, this depends on the speed and patience of the players. A fair way of arranging it is to allow as long as it takes for all but one player to write their definition, and then allow the last player no more than a minute extra.

Another convention followed in my circle, which may not appeal to all tastes, is that no one apart from the dictionary-holder should know the true definition of the word quoted.

When it is first announced, anyone who thinks he knows the meaning is called upon to give it, and if it is remotely right or likely to give a genuine pointer then it is replaced by another word. A certain degree of honesty is taken for granted here, but if everyone agrees that the game is better played this way they are unlikely to lie. There are those who think it more fun if a player does know the true meaning, whether he tries to throw others off the scent by defining the word as something completely different or to amuse them by writing a very similar definition, which is likely to add to their confusion. We have found that even if known words are omitted, players often come up with very similar definitions to the true one – and are still likely to vote for somebody else's in any case.

You are, of course, allowed to vote for your own definition. Like it or not, it is a fact that players tend to be influenced by one another's vote, especially if the one who votes first does so with the sort of confidence that comes from inside information. Voting for your own loses you the point for guessing the true definition (you *don't* get an extra point for choosing your own!) but may gain you two or three by convincing several players who are to vote after you. It is obviously best to do this from an early position in the voting hierarchy, though second rather than first, especially if the first player has already voted for your definition and so restored the point you lose for bluffing. Besides, a first-position bluff is too likely to be expected.

What happens if two definitions are word for word the same? Our rules are as follows. If one of them is the dictionary definition, those who vote for it score the point for a correct vote, while the dictionary-holder scores a point for each player who duplicated it. If not, each writer of a duplicated definition scores a point in respect of each opponent who votes for it.

Strategy You don't need me to point out that Fictionary tests your etymological skills. If a word is of obviously English origin, like *thrutch*, you are unlikely to be able to persuade anyone that it is a Polynesian sea-going vessel. Since it is obvious that *xylometer* has something to do with wood and something to do with measuring, you would be advised not to define it as a continuous sausage extruder. The lazy or beginner's way of approaching an imaginary definition is to assume that the word in question is a noun and that it denotes something foreign or at least dialectical. Avoid this by incorporating a fair share of verbs and adjectives in your compositions.

Apart from that, there is little that can usefully be said except to mention the very reason for not saying it: that Fictionary is essentially a game of bluff, and bluffing means above all changing your strategy in accordance with circumstances. Sometimes you will get away with the most preposterous definition simply because no one will believe that anyone would run the risk of losing points and that the ridiculous definition must therefore be the correct one. At other times you may get away with the most facile of definitions, which everyone else will have thought of and rejected as too obvious.

A large part of the skill, especially with the particular combination of rules and conventions followed by my circle, lies in reproducing the style of the dictionary and in spotting mannerisms of wording and thought processes which may give your opponents away. Perhaps I should have mentioned one vital rule which I may possibly have taken too much for granted: after each round the dictionary-holder must announce who wrote what, so that players may learn from their own and others' mistakes.

Fictionary is also an interesting test of general knowledge, specific knowledge and knowledge of one anothers' specialisms. If one player is an expert in or a fan of, say, chemistry, then it would be unwise for him to come up with chemical definitions which are so good as to give him away, or for others to attempt chemical definitions which are simply not good enough to fool the expert. In this respect, however, the dictionary-holder can have fun by selecting words that do relate to chemistry, as the others will then not be sure who is trying to bluff whom. A frequent occurrence is that a definition comes up which relates to a special subject and uses convincing terminology – let us say, 'doubly refracting, like Iceland spar' (the true definition of *birefringent*). This sets everybody wondering which member of the group is most likely to have sufficient acquaintance with optics and geology to have thought along such lines and been able to use convincing terminology to express the result. Good players will often invent plausible-sounding terms which are purely fictitious. Suppose the definition had been 'inversely refracting, like pentine crystal'. Do you know whether or not 'inversely refracting', which are known words individually, have any real meaning in combination? I don't. And I only know that 'pentine' is an invented word because I have just invented it.

The dictionary-holder can have as much fun as anybody and certainly has as much opportunity to bluff. Your object in this position is to fool the others into believing that the true definition is false. One way of doing this is to find a definition which sounds as if it were written by one of the other players, possibly because only one of the others would be suspected of thinking such a thing (see discussion on chemistry and geology above) or – more rarely – because the definition itself sounds awkwardly worded. Another is to find a word whose definition is too obvious, so as to make it sound as if one player's imagination is getting tired. A word I rather fancy for this purpose is *proleg*, which an alert and imaginative player might define as 'a pre-Bolshevik term for a member of the lowest class of serfdom', or possibly 'a false premiss assumed for the sake of logical argument'. I may well have voted for either of these in preference to the meaning given by *Chambers*: 'an insect larva's abdominal leg, distinguished from a thoracic or "true" leg'. It sounds simply too bad to be true!

No account of Fictionary Dictionary would be complete without some examples for you to work on in the bath, so here goes:

Crith means which of these?
  1. A flint shaped by nature but misleadingly resembling a palaeolithic tool.

2. A unit of mass, that of 1 litre at standard temperature and pressure.
3. Plural of *crwth*, a Welsh stringed instrument.
4. To shear a sheep partially, for decorative effect.

Eyra

1. A hermit's cave or other natural sanctuary.
2. In every direction; haphazardly (Scot.).
3. In Norse mythology, an attendant of the Valkyries.
4. A South American wild cat.

Mammee

1. A close female friend; confidante.
2. A highly esteemed fruit of the West Indies, having a sweet taste and aromatic odour.
3. Nickname for any 'blackface' singer (applied originally to Al Jolson).
4. One who was committed to Bedlam for political reasons.

Prog

1. A blanched sand soil, poor in humus.
2. Downward displacement, especially a drooping of the upper eyelid.
3. A pointed outcrop of rock on an otherwise grassy hillside.
4. To poke about for anything; to forage for food.

Zoster

1. An ancient Greek waist-belt for men.
2. A dish of wild oats, milk and honey.
3. A woven pattern similar to tartan but on a smaller scale.
4. Sister (dialectical).

For the true answers, see page 229.

Fabulary Vocabulary

Four to six players
Adults and older children
A game of competitive imaginations

Fictionary Dictionary does not have to be played with real words. If you start with purely imaginary words in the first place then you have the variation which cannot be called anything but Fabulary Vocabulary.

As before, the word-maker announces his word and everyone writes out a definition for it, which is passed on a slip to the word-maker. He then reads out all definitions including his own. Everybody including the word-maker votes for their preferred definition, which may not be their own. Furthermore, the votes must be made simultaneously or in secret, so that no one can be influenced by another's vote. The simplest way of doing this is to get everyone to write down the number of the definition they are voting for and then to reveal them when all players are ready.

Scores are not made for guessing the word-maker's definition but only for attracting other players' votes. Score 1 point for each player who chooses your definition. Alternatively (and in my view preferably) scale the scores up as follows: 1 vote scores you 1, 2 scores 3, 3 scores 6, 4 scores 10, etc.

I devised this variation so as to put to practical use a computer program I wrote which invents words. You can have the first twenty-six for nothing, together with my suggested meanings.

Antipavello: a tessellation of clay tiles in herring-bone pattern.

Binoctode: a poem recited twice nightly – or (erroneously) every two nights.

Coges: a bout of hard thinking, as in 'Don't disturb him – he's got the coges.'

Dogeer: a Venetian sycophant.

Elylamper: a Cardiff nightwatchman (pejorative).

Focery: an obscure Irish practice.

Gantiform: shaped like a glove.

Hodero: a Mexican bricklayer.

Isagron: a soap substitute derived from the intestines of seals.

Juminoce: sickly-sweet smelling, as of hyacinths past their prime.

Kaipe: a Greek delicacy consisting of fish cooked in sponge-cake.

Landop: where you might, if you're not careful.

Miserafin: a cheap and dangerous substitute for paraffin.

Nowit: in Yorkshire, an idiot ('no wit'); in Lancashire, a know-all ('(k)now it') (dial.).

Ovase: almost shaped like an egg, but not quite.

Pethod: a group of five, especially sheep (West-country dial.).

Quisato: one who does not know where he is going (usu. of operatic hero).

Ravimen: a diet of pasta and mineral water.

Sinsuan: having feet shaped like those of a monkey.

Transamontist: member of a Basque splinter-group opposed to everything.

Untutic: describing behaviour unworthy of a scholar and a gentleman, especially towards young female students.

Vollex: emotion leading to untutic behaviour.

Wilyn: wily, but unable to spell.

Xonk: conglomerate of matted hair and other stuff removed from waste-trap of bathroom sink.

Yeldon: nodley (backslang).

Ziman: a schoolboy confession (from 'It wuz 'im an' me, sir; *we* done it').

Encyclopedia Fictannica

Four to six players
Mainly for adults
A battle of wits

In the realm of fictionary games we soon discovered that even freer rein is given to the imagination by replacing the dictionary with an encyclopedia. *Britannica* may be going a bit far, as the entries are so long, but *Everyman's* can be confidently recommended for the purpose, and even the General Information section of *Pears Cyclopaedia* has been employed with great effect.

The rules of play are basically as for Fictionary Dictionary, except that the questionmaster is allowed to edit an entry if it seems over-long, though in our circle we don't approve of his rewriting it in his own style.

I shall always remember with amusement the first occasion on which we played this variation, although it was over ten years ago – which is just as well, since I have (uncharacteristically) lost from my files the original slips of paper on which we played it. One of the first entries we were called upon to explain was *Levant et couchant*, and I will reproduce as best I can the four explanations given of this term. In alphabetical order of opening words, they were (more or less):

1. French equivalent of 'bed and breakfast'; obsolete in its original sense since employed by Parisian anarchists of the 1860s to describe those of their number who had been seized and held without trial; hence a generic term for imprisonment in such circumstances.

2. Picturesque term coined during the Napoleonic era to refer to the Mediterranean Sea, presumably inspired by the sight of the sun *levant* at its eastern and *couchant* at its western extremity.

3. The right to distrain cattle which, having strayed on to one's own land, have remained there long enough to have risen to graze and settled to rest at least once – in effect, for one whole day.

4. Type of comedians' 'double act' once popular in the French music halls, characterized by knockabout routines (one comedian falling down whilst the other was rising to his feet) and often leading into a free-for-all apache dance.

The particularly amusing thing about this entry is that each of the false entries received one vote and no one spotted the truth. (Can you do better? See page 229 to check.) I only wish I had not mislaid our efforts at explaining or defining the Plug Riots – I can't even find the reference book containing the entry. But, browsing vainly through *Pears* in search of it, I am reminded that the Encyclopedia Game, more so than the Dictionary game, lends itself well to entries which players know *more or less* but not exactly. It is very hard to choose between four or five marginally different definitions of, say, the Master of the Revels or Kew Gardens.

Whose Who's Who?

Four to six players
Mainly for adults
Another battle of wits

More fun along Fictionary lines may be had with a *Who's Who* or that twentieth-century almanack, the Prominent People section of good old *Pears*. Each questionmaster in turn picks a 'prominent person' – it makes no difference whether heard of or not heard of by the players, though it is better if they *all* either do or do not know the subject – and everybody writes an appropriate potted biography, which need not be more than one line if the prominent person is or is claimed to be undetailed by historians.

To give you the flavour of this variant, here are some accounts of one Rosa Bonheur. By way of a change, these are in order of supposed dates of birth.

1. (1822–99) A native of Bordeaux, and one of the most noted animal painters of the nineteenth century.

2. (1840–99) A follower of Florence Nightingale, whose nursing service she adopted and developed during the Franco-Prussian War. An award made in her name in times of war was last presented in 1958.
3. (1884–1914) Belgian soprano associated with a revival of interest in French folk songs. Died in mysterious circumstances following rumours of a liaison with the composer Claude Debussy.
4. (1903–   ) Viennese film actress famed for historical roles but who failed to make a successful transition to talking pictures.

True answer on page 229.

This game is particularly vicious when the subject is still alive and well known, especially a politician.

Blind Dates

Four to six players
Mainly for adults
An historical contest

Pears also contains a section in chronological order entitled simply Events. The question-master accordingly picks a year and everybody has to invent a plausible series of historical events associated with it. This section is such a ragbag of bits and pieces of unrelated rubbish that even the true answers sound invented. For instance, what *really* happened in 1493?

1. Columbus returns from first voyage to America. Second Battle of St Albans.
2. First printing of Papal indulgences, Nuremberg.
3. Henry VII calls reconstituted parliament. Icelandic traders recolonize Greenland.
4. Sonni Ali brings Songhai Empire to height of its prestige: Timbuktu renowned centre of literary culture.

For the least false answer, see page 229.

Captions Courageous

Four to six players
Adults and older children
Fun, but advance preparation needed

I name this game (and good luck to all who sail in her) after a couple of amusing books of the same title by Bob Reisner dating from the fifties. Reisner developed a superb knack of attaching imaginary but suitable captions or quotations to famous paintings, and his books merely consisted of reproductions of the paintings – or, in some cases, statues or sculptures – with captions attached. To pick a few well-known examples:

1. Sir Joshua Reynolds's *Miss Emily Pott as Thais*: a nymph in an obvious hurry and bearing a flaming torch aloft: 'The fuse box is over here.'
2. Nicholas Hilliard's *Portrait Miniature* – a pretty young man surrounded by roses and leaning against a tree: 'I refuse to read my sonnets to jazz.'
3. Myron's *Discobolus*, Rome: 'I asked for monaural, not stereophonic.'
4. Rubens's *Judgement of Paris* (though any other artist's rendering would probably do as well): 'I have the right to cancel my membership after making six club choices.'
5. My favourite – Millet's *The Gleaners*: 'On your mark, get set, go.'

Otherwise, however, there is not a great deal of resemblance. For my version of Captions Courageous you need some advance preparation, preferably by everybody concerned.

Each player should come equipped with several blank sheets of paper, on each of which has been mounted an illustration cut out from a newspaper or magazine. It may be a photograph or drawing, even a diagram or map, though pictures of people tend to inspire the funniest results. Each picture should be associated with its genuine printed caption, though the caption should not appear on the same sheet as the picture. (In our group each player sticks all his captions on one sheet of paper for ease of reference.)

The course of the game will by now be apparent. Each player in turn passes one of his pictures around the group and writes out the genuine caption on the usual slip of paper. The others then invent suitable captions of their own and pass them to the quizzer, who, as usual, reads them out to be voted on. (See Fictionary Dictionary for rules and scoring.)

Captions Courageous gives probably more scope to the imagination than any other member of the Fictionary family. One of the skills of the game lies in guessing the identity of the newspaper or magazine from which the picture comes, since that will give you some idea of a suitable style to write in and will help you judge others' efforts by the same criterion.

A major delight of the game is the not infrequent instance of a carefully chosen caption which is ambiguous, misleading or even positively mistaken. In one of our games, for instance, a player showed a picture purportedly depicting a well-camouflaged butterfly in suitable surroundings. The true caption (I quote from memory) was something like: 'The butterfly is the patch of lighter orange near the bottom left corner.' This gave everyone much food for thought, chiefly because the picture was actually reproduced in black and white. Which was more likely – that the original caption-writer had made a mistake (or been double-crossed at production stage) or that one of the other players had had a mental aberration? Or was one of the other players running a double bluff? I only wish I could remember the outcome of this particular gaffe.

A more successful example was culled from the *Radio Times*. It was a still from *A Day at the Races*, and one of the captions we were faced with dated the film to 1938. As it happens, all the players could be expected to know that the true date was 1937, though one could conceivably have been hazy about this. So was one player hazy or had the *Radio Times* got it wrong? We all assumed the former, and the quizzer made a nice score. The true caption *was* false.

Suspended Sentences

Four to six players
Mainly for adults
A game of deep concentration

Another one of my Fictionary variants, this was first published in *Games & Puzzles* and was later given its better title by Ross Eckler in the same publication. It is more difficult than any of the preceding games and requires a fair amount of thinking time.

The quizzer chooses a short sentence from a book, preferably a novel by a well-known author, and announces the initial letters of the constituent words. The other players then have to invent sentences whose words begin with the same sequence of initials as the original. As you would expect, the quizzer reads them all out, in alphabetical order, including the genuine one, and players have to spot the original.

One problem with this game is that any sequence of more than about ten letters is very difficult to transform into a likely-sounding sentence, but on the other hand it isn't easy to find such short sentences in the works of most writers. The quizzer is not, therefore, obliged to pick a sentence which begins with a capital letter and ends with a full point, but may pick out any genuine sequence of words containing a main verb. For example, take the following passage from Dickens (*Our Mutual Friend*):

'The Secretary thought, as he glanced at the schoolmaster's face, that he had opened a channel here indeed, and that it was an unexpectedly dark and deep and stormy one, and difficult to sound.'

From this it would be legitimate to extract H G A T S F ('He glanced at the schoolmaster's face'), or H H O A C H I ('He had opened a channel here indeed'), or I W A U D A D A S O ('It was an unexpectedly dark and deep and stormy one'). I would not even object to T S T A H G A T S F: 'The secretary thought as he glanced at the schoolmaster's face'. But you could certainly not have A H G A T S F – 'As he glanced at the schoolmaster's face' is obviously only a subordinate clause, i.e. it could not stand as a complete sentence by itself with an initial capital and terminal full point.

These examples may well mislead you into believing the game is easier than it looks. Once you know what the letters stand for the real sentence seems obvious, not to say inevitable. But now try it without any further clue but that the following comes from the same book (answer on page 229):

H E O T H O T F M
1. Has everyone observed the habits of the frugal master?
2. He entered on the history of the friendly move.
3. He expects one tenth: helmsmen only talk for money.
4. Have everything, only take half on trust for me.
5. Hope, expectation of the hoard opened their fecund mouths.
6. How execrable – only the head of the family matters!

In choosing sentences, bear in mind that certain initials are easier to turn into words than others. The table on page 224 may be found useful in this respect.

It is advisable to avoid sentences containing any of the six least frequent letters as initials, and not more than two of the preceding group of five should appear in the same passage – unless you really have all the time in the world for playing the game.

Ross Eckler proposes a variant on Suspended Sentences, in which, instead of giving the initial letters of the constituent words, you quote a string of figures indicating their length. Thus 'He glanced at the schoolmaster's face' would be given as 2, 7, 2, 3, 13, 4. I haven't played this version yet but imagine it might be easier to compose suitable sentences. If so, they can be longer than in the parent game.

Deductive games played with pencil and paper are generally more advanced and brain-storming than those performed orally, as described earlier, though a simple start may be made with Anagrams and Hangman.

Anagrams

Any number of players
Mainly for children
A fairly controllable party game

All word-gamers love anagrams. It is perhaps because anagrams lie at the root of so many popular games that they remain popular for generation after generation of games-players. Most crossword puzzles include a higher proportion of anagrams than any other single type of clue, and the weekly puzzle mags abound in anagrams of one sort or another. The pleasure of solving an anagram is probably less the arrival at the solution than the process of getting there, as you juggle letters around in your mind's eye and come up with all sorts of intriguing combinations which look as if they ought to be words, even if they aren't.

Many of the games in this book involve some sort of anagramming, though the solution of the anagram itself is not the main point of the game: for competitive purposes it has to be a means rather than an end in itself. But this need not be the case where children are concerned. Puzzling over anagrams appeals enough to children to make a good party game, provided that they are not made too difficult, and I dare say it would be easy to argue that a degree of educational value may be derived from it. ('Educational value' is so often glibly claimed for toys and games that I sometimes wonder if it isn't all too good to be true.)

To make anagrams workable as a party game and suitable for children the words concerned should be of picturable objects, preferably all of the same class or category, such as birds, flowers, seaside objects, tools and so on. To make them at the same time interesting, even amusing, don't just put down the first jumble of letters that come into your head, but try to make something pronounceable or even other words out of them.

Make about ten anagrams on the same topic and print each one neatly on a separate card – about the size of a postcard – in 'small' letters rather than capitals. Dot them around the room so that children have the additional activity of walking around finding them; otherwise what is meant to be a game will turn out to be more like an old-fashioned school examination. Explain that what they have to do is to find and write down the names of ten flowers (or whatever) by unscrambling the letters on each card. If you can give yet further help by providing illustrations of the anagrammed objects, so much the better.

The following anagrammed flowers would be suitable for children with a reading age of about ten. Notice that they make nonsense words wherever possible rather than unpronounceable jumble. You don't need the answers, do you?

A I D H A L
F O D D L I A F
L U L L B E E B
P O R M I S E R
R A M L I D O G
S C O U R C
S L O W E R F U N
T O L I V E
U P T I L
W O R N P O D S

Hangman

Two players, really, but any number can take part
Mainly for children
A fast and not too demanding exercise

Nothing new strikes me to say about this classic word game,
which at least one manufacturer has turned into a proprietary
boxed game, so short are they getting of new ideas.

One player – let us call him the hangman – thinks of a word
and draws a line of dots or dashes, one for each letter of the
word he has in mind. The other player or players (the
'hangees'?) have thirteen chances of finding out what the word
is. Each of them in turn calls out a letter of the alphabet. If
the word contains that letter, the hangman fills it in in the
appropriate space of the word – or spaces, if it occurs more
than once. If it does not contain the chosen letter, the hangman
draws in one part of the following figure, which, as you will
see, contains exactly thirteen separate bits. (It doesn't matter
which bits you put in. Some people give the hanged man eyes
instead of feet, for example. But the details of the drawing are
not important, so long as there are thirteen of them.)

If the word is correctly guessed before the drawing is completed then the hangees have won; conversely, the hangman wins if he completes it before the word is guessed. The hangman also wins if a word is guessed and proves incorrect, though in this case some players prefer just to mark up another piece of the drawing.

Hangman can be made a little more interesting by awarding points and declaring as winner the player with the highest total at the end of a given number of games, or the first player to reach a given target score. Thus the hangman, if he wins, scores 1 point for each part of the drawing he has managed to complete – that is, 13 if the word is not guessed, or a smaller number if his turn ends with a wrong guess made. His opponent scores, for winning, 13 minus the number of bits of drawing made by the time he guesses correctly.

If more than two play, the player who correctly guesses the word scores for it as just described. If a wrong guess is made, the Hangman adds another bit of the drawing and scores 1 point for each section so far completed, but play continues until either the word is discovered or the drawing is completed.

The hangman may be required to write down his secret word on a hidden piece of paper before play begins and to reveal it at the end of his turn, as a guard against one or two things about the game which have been known to go wrong in the past.

Hangman is a very good game for improving children's literacy. Younger players at first tend to choose letters haphazardly but with further experience begin to discover that words are inclined to follow certain patterns – for example, that something ending in G‑T often has an H in the middle, or that U may well be preceded by Q. They will also soon discover that shorter words are generally harder to deduce than longer ones, simply because there are so many possibilities. How many three-letter words, for example, are of the form - - Y?

Younger children may be allowed to make a note of the

letters they have called so as not to lose by calling the same ones twice. Hangman is a game of deduction, not memory.

Jotto or Giotto

Two players
Adults and older children
A battle of wits

I have been playing this game since the earliest known times – i.e., as far back as I can remember – without becoming aware until recently that it had a name, let alone several variations with a name for each. It is the verbal equivalent of a pencil-and-paper number game known to me as Bull and Cow, and of Meirovits's coloured pegs deductive game published under the title Mastermind.

Each player writes down a key word of agreed length – let us say five letters. The object is to be the first to deduce the opponent's word from information provided in accordance with the following method of play.

Each player in turn calls out a five-letter test word. The opponent then states how many letters of the test word appear in his key word, regardless of position. For example:

Keyword ENEMY

Tests ABOUT = 0: no letters in common with ENEMY

MINER = 3: M, N and E in common

TENET = 3: an N and two Es in common

These are not very typical test words (though zero for the first one is a good result as it safely eliminates five) but are chosen to illustrate how correspondences are to be counted. Thus, although there are two Es in the key word, only one correspondence is counted for the test word MINER. With TENET, however, each E of the test word can be paired off with an E of the key word, making two correspondences.

The winner is the first to call a test word which proves to be the key word.

Jotto may be played with any agreed length of word. I prefer five letters. Four is somewhat restrictive as to variety of key words possible, while six makes for a shorter and easier game because the amount of information deriving from possible six-letter correspondences is significantly larger than for five.

Some players forbid anagrams. For example, if the key word is STONE, then NOTES, with five correspondences, would win. The argument in favour of this rule is that it keeps Jotto a deductive game instead of to some extent a guessing game, but I find this rather dull and purist. I have before now had some success with the combination that produces STONE, NOTES and TONES, all of them being tried as test words and none of them being the true key word, which I will leave you to work out for yourself.

Strategy In choosing a key word you might bear in mind that words with repeated letters are generally more difficult to deduce than words which are completely heteroliteral, though an opponent may be lucky enough to spot the repetition and come up with a suitable test word. In the case of ENEMY above, for example, the first three test words were not theoretically well chosen but in the event happen to have yielded very promising information.

For instance, the first word, ABOUT, produced a score of zero. This not only eliminates five different letters from consideration as part of the key word but also enables two or more of them to be used in subsequent test words with the promise of more useful information to come. A continuation such as EBONY would have given a score of three correspondences, confirming the appearance of E, N and Y in the keyword, since B and O have been eliminated.

The most unhelpful information is usually that of one or two correspondences. Thus three for both the second and third words of the example above was particularly helpful. Since T has been eliminated because of ABOUT, the three correspondences of TENET must be E, E, N, while the result for MINER

shows that one of the other two letters is M, I or R. A handy
way of recording this information on a spare piece of paper is
as follows:

E E N M .

I

R

This reminds you that M, I and R are mutually exclusive for
one letter of the key word: if one of them is in, the other two
must be out. The dot shows that you have as yet no clue as to
the fifth letter.

If your first test words yield three or more correspondences
on average it is worth working away at similar combinations of
letters. More usually, however, the first few words produce
one or two apiece. In this case I find it useful to let my first half
dozen words include between them as many of the twenty-six
letters as possible. If one of them gives a score of zero I will be
very happy, since they can then be used as known letters in
subsequent test words.

If you do come up with a test word yielding five correspondences, making an anagram of the keyword concerned, the
obvious thing to do is work out all possible words and then
decide which one your opponent is most likely to have thought
you least likely to have guessed first. This is not so much luck
as a matter of bluff.

As a puzzle before leaving this subject, can you find five
words which between them exhaust twenty-five letters of the
alphabet? Two solutions appear on page 229. They include
some pretty obscure words, but one list is supported by
Chambers and the other by *Webster's Second Unabridged
Dictionary*.

Double Jeopardy

Two players
Adults and older children
A battle of wits

An excellent variation on the rules of Jotto, also applicable to similar target-word deductive games such as Crash, has recently been proposed by Australian games expert Don Laycock under the title Double Jeopardy.

In this system, each time a player calls a test word he must also announce how many correspondences it makes with his *own* target word. Thus the quest for information can only be made at the expense of yielding information about one's own target. Considerably more skill is called for in devising test words which stand to gain maximum information about your opponent's target while admitting the minimum about your own.

Crash

Two players
Adults and older children
A concentrated game

This variant of Jotto is somewhat harder and therefore takes longer to play. A *crash* is a correspondence between letters in the same position in both test word and key word. In Crash, you are told only the number of crashes, not the number of correspondences. Thus for the key word ENEMY the test words ABOUT, MINER and TENET would all score zero crashes, since none of them has E in the first position, N in the second and so on. EBONY, on the other hand, would score two for E and Y.

Wild Crash

Two players
Mainly for adults
A complex game requiring thinking time

Either Crash or Jotto may be played 'wild', which introduces the following feature: a player may keep changing his key word, so long as he does not thereby change any of the information already given. As will be seen from the following example, this is easier to do for Crash than for Jotto and for shorter rather than longer words. The chief problem lies in coordinating all the information already given without making a mistake.

Suppose the first player starts with the key word TANK. The second tries MAKE and gets one crash. He next tries TAKE, which ought to be two crashes. But now the first player changes his key word to LAMP and announces only one crash, which we know is still the A in second position.

As you can see, the first player is eventually going to run out of different key words to change to (he may not use the same one twice) and the second will eventually pin him down to a complete correspondence of crashes. But it will take a long time.

Convergence

Two players
Mainly for adults
A more enjoyable variation

Rather a dull title for a really advanced but amusing member of the Jotto family.

Each player writes a four-word sentence, which the other seeks to deduce first. Each in turn announces a test sentence of four words. For each word of the test sentence, the opponent states whether it precedes or follows the equivalent word in the key sentence when considered in dictionary or alphabetical order.

Suppose, for example, the key sentence is

MY DOG HAS FLEAS

The first test sentence is GET YOUR SKATES ON. The information given in response is 'After, before, before, before', since MY comes alphabetically after GET, while DOG is before YOUR, HAS is before SKATES and FLEAS before ON. No doubt you will think of more convenient words to call out than 'before' and 'after' to achieve the same effect. I favour 'up' if the equivalent key word is further up the dictionary and 'down' if lower on the alphabetical list.

If this goes on too long you may agree to shorten it by announcing when a word in the test sentence has the same initial as the equivalent word in the key sentence.

Three words is too short for a reasonable sentence; five makes for an extremely long game.

Quizl

Two players
Adults and older children
A contest of perception

This two-dimensional deductive game is of my own invention and has not previously been published, though it is quite closely related to Get the Message, which has.

Method Each player draws a grid of $5 \times 5 = 25$ squares and numbers the columns 1 to 5 (or 0 to 4) along the top and 6 to 0 (or 5 to 9) down one side. The numbering is to enable individual squares to be identified, as in the game of Battleships – for example, the middle square will be known as 38 or 83, or 27 or 72 depending on how you happen to number things. (I always start with 0.)

Into any row or column of your grid (but not diagonal) you now enter a key word whose five letters are all different. If entered in a column, it must be written from top to bottom, if in a row, from left to right. Your opponent meanwhile does likewise; the object of the game, of course, is to cleverly deduce his key word before he is lucky enough to guess your own.

This leaves you with twenty unfilled spaces and twenty-one unused letters. What more natural continuation than to fill up the rest of the square with twenty of the spare letters? Go ahead – but make sure that (a) no letter appears twice in the whole thing and (b) no other row or column contains a genuine five-letter word. This last point is very important, since much of the strategy depends on it. Only one genuine five-letter word may appear in the grid; ideally, all the other rows and columns are filled with five-letter *quizls*. A quizl – possibly so called because it is a cross between a piz and a quuzzle – is a five-letter combination which looks as if it might be going to be a five-letter word when you can only see three or four of them. It might even be a genuine three- or four-letter word with a rubbish letter attached to it – like QUIZL itself.

The rest of the game will now be obvious to dedicated gamesters. Each player in turn, having previously drawn a second grid and left it blank, calls out a particular square by means of its grid references. The opponent announces what letter occupies that square; the caller then enters this into his spare grid so as to build up a gradual picture of the opposing pattern.

Instead of calling a grid reference, you may use your turn to announce what you think your opponent's word is. If correct, you score 1 point for each square of his grid which has not so far been called or identified. (Or, to put it the other way, score 25 minus the number of 'shots' you have fired.) This ends the round, unless you both enjoy the game so much that you wish to continue until the loser has similarly deduced the winner's word, in which case I suggest that the winner scores twice his number of unfired shots and the loser once his number.

There is no penalty for a wrong guess, beyond the fact that you lose your 'shot' for that turn.

If you entirely uncover your opponent's word – all five letters of it – you score nothing. The point of the game is to deduce it, not strip it.

If either player eventually proves to have included two genuine five-letter words in his grid, which can happen if he is not aware that a particular combination is in fact not a quizl but a word, he scores nothing for the round; his opponent wins as soon as he correctly announces either of them.

Variation I Instead of calling out references, you might try calling out letters and being informed which squares they occupy. I haven't tried this version: it seems workable, but I think it may be less interesting. (If you try it, let me know how you get on.)

Variation II Another variation I haven't tried, since it strikes me as horrendously difficult, is to enter the key word as an anagram – i.e., correctly filling a row or column but with its letters in any order.

Strategy One could make out a case for claiming three skills to be at play in Quizl.

The first one is hitting on a suitable key word to start with. This is where the advance preparation comes in. Regular players are heard to complain: 'I came across a terrific five-letter word for Quizl the other day, only I've forgotten it.' The only answer to this is to write them down and save them up. Otherwise, when you come to play, all you can think of is the most obvious five-letter words like *think* or *psalm* or *quoin*. A really good key word is one which looks impossible from only a couple of letters. One that fooled me completely once was - U - J - . Having uncovered that much of the row or column in question, I decided it could not conceal the true key word and so failed to fire any more shots into it. Can you work it out? (The answer does not appear on page 229. Nor does it appear on any other in this book.)

Much ingenuity can also be applied to arranging the other twenty letters in the square. It is not good enough to allow all your quizls to be haphazard jumbles of letters. Wherever possible, letters should be placed together that often go together in making up words. A good place for a Y, for instance, is at the end of a word, and a good letter to precede it is L, since no one can safely pass a line appearing as - - - L Y without firing another shot into it. It is true that the placing of three of J, Q, X and Z (since one of them can be omitted entirely from the grid) causes problems in this respect, but the usual method of dealing with them is to put all the letters together in the same row or column, thus revealing only one obvious 'junk' line rather than several.

A typical filled-in grid might conceal the keyword PSALM as follows:

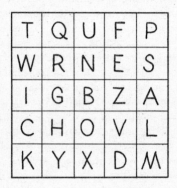

Note, for instance, that all nine letters at the ends of rows and columns are common 'end' letters; that R is a good second letter; that common digrams such as QU, NE, ES, CH, OV, GH, UN and BO appear; and that TWICK and UNBOX could easily be genuine words – in fact, there could be argument over UNBOX: though not listed in *Chambers*'s long list of UN-words, it could well be spontaneously used and understood as meaning 'to take out of its box'. The *OED* also lists TWICK as obsolete or dialectical for TWITCH, but I doubt if many players would be knowledgeable enough to challenge it.

This grid was compiled in accordance with the following principles. First, consider the word PSALM. Its constituent letters are all common as finals, so the word is best placed along the bottom or down the right-hand side. It uses only one vowel, so the next step is to enter the other five (including Y) in suitable spaces to ensure that one appears in every row and column, for no opponent will leave unmolested a row with a vowel in it unless its neighbours are obvious junk. Then fill in some of the awkward letters: Q goes with U and is most likely to appear at the start of a word, or in second position after (say) E or S. Letter X follows O quite well; K and C can go hand in hand at the end of a quizl; and so on.

The ultimate skill lies in unearthing possible word patterns as you gradually fill in your record of the opposing square, in eliminating possibilities by considering which letters have already gone, and in choosing shots that will yield maximal useful information. One early objective is to get good coverage of the square by placing your first five shots in different rows and columns; a second is to keep track of the vowels. In the latter connection I think it generally unwise to make word guesses until the position of all vowels is known. After some experience of the game you will be very alert to common digrams. For instance, wherever there is a U remember it might be preceded by Q (Q-words are not uncommon in quizl); wherever N is a second letter, think of words that begin with UN (a favourite key word of mine is UNWED), and remain alert to that possibility so long as you fail to uncover the real position of the U; bear in mind that H can be preceded in almost any position by a variety of consonants; and so on.

Get the Message

Two players
Adults and older children
Another perceptive game

Like Quizl, to which it is clearly related, Get the Message is another game of my invention first published in *Games & Puzzles* magazine. It has since been described, by someone else, under the name Phrase Maze.

Each player draws a grid of 5 × 5 = 25 squares and numbers the rows and columns, as in Quizl or Battleships.

Think of a well-known phrase, saying or title (of book, film, etc.) of up to twenty-five letters, and enter its constituent letters into the grid in such a way as to follow a pathway of adjacent squares. For example, you might write HE WHO HESITATES IS LOST starting half way down the right-hand side:

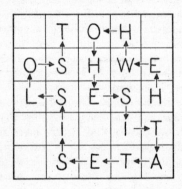

The object is for each to deduce the other's message first by taking it in turns to fire shots at stated squares, being told either what letter occupies a stated square or that the square is blank. At any turn you may make a guess at the hidden message instead of potting at a square.

Each time you hit a blank you score a point. (This encourages players to think of messages that fill as many squares as possible.) Each time you make a wrong guess at the message your opponent scores a point. Whoever correctly guesses the other's message first scores an additional point for each square of the message which he has not yet shot at (unpotted blanks do not count) and the round ends.

You can play the game on a larger grid so as to accommodate longer titles, messages, proverbs or quotations.

Foreheads

Four to six players
Mainly for adults
Concentrated, but amusing

First described by Dave Silverman in the November 1974 edition of *Word Ways*, Foreheads features deduction with a vengeance.

Each player writes a four-letter word neatly and largely on a self-adhesive label, about 4×2 cm, and sticks it on the forehead of the player on his right without showing him what the word is. The object is to be the first to discover one's own forehead word, or foreword, as I would have called it if I'd thought of the game myself. This object is to be achieved in the following way.

Each player in turn announces a word which must be four letters in length and may not contain any letter which the caller cannot see on a forehead. Or, when he thinks he knows his own word, he may instead use his turn to announce what he thinks it is. He wins the round if the word he guesses is either correct or an anagram of the true word – that is to say, the object is really to discover the four letters on one's own forehead, not necessarily the word they make. If the guess is wrong he remains in the game but has lost, since he may not guess again.

Repeated letters are allowed both on the forehead labels and in the clue word stated at each turn. The same clue word may not be called twice. If a player cannot think of a different clue word he has lost and may not guess his own foreword.

By way of illustration, let us suppose players 1 to 5 have the following words attached to them: (1) HELP, (2) FIEF, (3) CZAR, (4) NOON, (5) TALC. The first clue-words might be:

1. CANT (from which player 4 knows he has an N, player 5 a T)
2. LATE (from which player 1 can deduce an E in his word)
3. NEAT (giving nothing away that I can see)
4. TELL
5. LACE (from which player 1 learns about his L)

. . . and so on. From this you will note the importance of avoiding clue words containing letters you can see on only one forehead; no one, for instance, has let slip any reference to F, H, P or Z yet.

(My wife has just asked me why I am sitting here with the word HELP labelled to my forehead. The answer is that I have been testing the efficacy of self-adhesive labels as an alternative to the use of ordinary labels and sticky tape quoted in the original source. I think I can safely say that self-adhesive labels are more comfortable.)

Postscripts

Acceptability of words in word games

Word games differ from most other games in a distinctive double feature which can be either charming or exasperating, depending on which barrel is loaded and which end of it you happen to be facing at the time. This is the question as to whether a given sequence of letters does or does not exist as a word, and, if so, whether it should be acceptable as such in a given word game.

If you were learning Poker, you would be told that a 'full house' is a hand containing three cards of one rank plus two of another. Thereafter, if dealt (say) three Sixes and two Kings, you would be in no doubt that you held a full house. If you were an alien learning English word games, you might be told that a word can begin with CH, that CH can be followed by EA, and that EAL is a possible word ending. Thereafter, confronted with CHEAL – you would not be any the wiser as to whether it were a word or not. CHEAL is only a word if it has a meaning. WHEAL has a meaning; so does CHEAT; so even does WHEAT. But CHEAL? (Come to think of it, what is a meaning anyway?)

Any three cards of one rank and two of another make a full house, but the combination of any three consonants and two vowels only makes a word if it happens to be assigned a 'meaning' in a quite haphazard list of letter-combinations known as a 'dictionary'. It is this asymmetry or unpredictability of the material that makes word games so appealing (or appalling, if you're at the wrong end of the barrel). Words defy logic. So do most people. Hence the popularity of word games.

But it is an irregularity that can hinder the enjoyment of word games by causing arguments. How can this problem be overcome?

One way is to agree beforehand that words only count if they are listed in the nearest dictionary to hand. This may be called the Rule of Authority. Even as it stands, it causes complications due to the fact that dictionaries not only differ from one another as to which words they have the space or inclination to recognize but also tend to be inconsistent within their own covers. For instance, *Chambers Twentieth Century Dictionary*, widely used by British word-gamers, lists some interjections but not others, recognizes the verb *cuddle* but not the adjective *cuddly*, and writes *Swede* (the vegetable) as if it were a personal name. In any case, word-gamers do not normally restrict themselves to dictionary words but go further by refusing to recognize certain categories, such as unnaturalized foreign words, words spelt with a capital initial and the verbal forms of letters of the alphabet.

Thus the Rule of Authority is bad in principle, because it wrongly assumes that the language is fixed and immutable, and bad in practice, if only because it is abused.

In its place, therefore, I wish to propose the Rule of Appeal. This does not do away with dictionaries, but relegates them to a position of last resort. It throws the responsibility of word recognition on to the players themselves. To be effective, it requires players to make disinterested judgements which may conflict with their own positions at the time of appeal. This may cause problems among players with an overdeveloped sense of competitiveness, and therefore cannot be recommended to their attention: they will be better off with the more dogmatic Rule of Authority. It has always proved effective in my circle of players. It runs as follows:

RULE OF APPEAL

A word is acceptable if (a) it exists, (b) it is spelt correctly, and (c) it accords with the conventions of the game. If a word is challenged under any of these heads the claimant may appeal to the other players. If at least one opponent accepts it, then it is acceptable. If not, the claimant must either withdraw it or win support by using a dictionary or other source to demonstrate the word's existence, spelling or conformity with agreed conventions.

Obviously, in a two-player game there is likely to be more emphasis on recourse to printed references than when more are taking part. However, the principle should still be as far as possible that language was made for man and not man for language: dictionaries can only follow and lag behind the usage of speakers, to which they should be regarded as standing in subservience rather than authority.

In applying the Rule of Appeal, a dictionary can be used to demonstrate that a word 'exists'. The dictionary may list it as a main or subsidiary entry or draw attention to it in some other way. If not flatly contradicted by the dictionary, the word may be inferrable from a main entry by application of the normal rules of English word-construction. For example, nouns are pluralized by the addition of S unless otherwise stated – e.g. the listing of CHILDREN as the plural of CHILD negates the form CHILDS. But even here dictionaries will let you down. From *Chambers*, for instance, you can infer *ifs* and *buts* but not *whys* and *wherefores*.

Words may be omitted from dictionaries for many reasons. The simplest is that there are so many words that only the largest could seek to list them all: the shorter they are, the more they must omit. What might be called source dictionaries, such as the *Oxford English*, support their material by quotations from literature in which the various words and their forms have been used. Such works take years to compile and are out of date by the time they appear. Newer dictionaries may make some use of real sources but seek primarily to up-date existing material ultimately derived from source dictionaries.

In these circumstances it seems reasonable to allow players to support claimed words by reference to primary sources. In other words, if you can demonstrate that the word or form of word which you are claiming has been used in print in an intelligible way, and without attention being drawn to it as a coinage, that should be sufficient to persuade an opponent to deem it 'acceptable'. This resource should be used with discretion – or, at least, with a time limit; otherwise the burden of proof could hold the game up by going on all night.

Another way of seeking support for a claimed word is to propose a fluent sentence which contains it naturally and intelligibly and without drawing attention to itself as a coinage. This applies especially to words formed by the addition of affixes such as RE-, UN-, -MENT, -IZATION, etc. I would not expect any dictionary to list *unvowed*, for instance, but cannot find any objection to its use in a sentence such as 'The candidate left no electoral promise unvowed.'

Similar remarks apply to the question of spelling, but with provisos. A general proviso is that players should agree beforehand whether to accept both British and American alternative spellings or only those applicable to themselves. On the whole I favour the latter, though it could give rise to problems in mixed British and American company. Other alternative spellings may be accepted if listed in the dictionary. Otherwise, however, it is not wise to go to primary sources. Many a journalist commits such spelling errors as *supercede*, *forsee*, *ancilliary* and so on, and even books have been known to contain mirsprints. As for proposing a sentence containing your own spelling . . . I spoze you could try it on, but don't expect it to be accepted. The spelling of words is more open to authority than their existence. Spellings are conventional rather than natural, and their maintenance is a matter of practical desirability rather than élitist tyranny. Written communication would break down if we all spelt as the fancy took us.

The third part of my Rule of Appeal – accordance with the conventions of acceptability – recognizes the fact that most players agree to count certain types of words as unacceptable, though different circles rarely agree as to which categories they ban. One extremist school of thought maintains that word games should test only one's active vocabulary, i.e. those words which players themselves are likely to have used in context over the past year. In my case this would cut out such unexceptional words as *jeopardy* and *coax*, which I am quite convinced I have not used in the past ten years, if ever. (That is to say, ten years ago it occurred to me to wonder if I had ever used them; since then I have been keeping a careful watch but have never found myself in a context where either word would be the most natural choice.) A literate person's passive vocabulary will contain many more words which he recognizes than he is likely to use. Even so, there are certain words which seem to have any active existence only in word games – things like *al* and *jo* and *zax* – and I for one would be quite happy to ban them if it were at all possible to draw a sensible dividing line between a vocabulary active only in games and a passively communicative one. The only practical way of doing this, however, would be to restrict play to the use of no more than the 850 words of Ogden's 'Basic English' vocabulary, as promoted during the 1930s as an international auxiliary language. But this would probably not make for a wildly exciting game of any sort.

I share most players' desire to avoid words which exist only as proper names and have some sympathy with their dislike of not-yet-naturalized foreign words. I cannot understand the objection to 'slang', or to the verbal forms of letters of the alphabet – *aitch* and *ar*, to name two – but dare say that many would not share my aversion to interjections in general and those of two letters, such as *fy* and *st*, in particular. (If you're having *st*, I want *zz*.) Indeed, I would do away with two-letter words altogether: some games would improve immeasurably as a result.

The trouble with any proposed rule to allow or disallow certain types of word is that lines have to be drawn somewhere, but words do not fit into logically circumscribed categories capable of such delineation. If rules are interpreted by the spirit, opposing players will disagree because of human nature. If they are interpreted by the letter, such absurdities occur as the recent ruling of the British National Scrabble Championships permitting the plural forms of interjections. *Ahs* may just about pass muster ('This prospect was greeted with many oohs and ahs'), but, really, would you seriously allow *shs*?

It may be amusing, even instructive, to see what other problems and absurdities can arise from the various criteria of acceptability open to adoption by word-gamers.

Names 'They are the most economical of all words', declares Sir Alan Gardiner in *The Theory of Proper Names*, 'inasmuch as they make only a very small demand on the eloquence of the speaker, and an equally small demand upon the attention of the listener.'

A clever remark, and, like most clever remarks, highly debatable. If I were listening to a speech in which I was enjoined to show the qualities of a Codrus I should feel that a very great demand was being made upon my attention, and obliged forthwith to consult my copy of Betty Radice's invaluable *Who's Who in the Ancient World*. Gardiner was evidently no word-gamer; otherwise he would have realized that it is precisely because they make too great a demand on the attention that most players refuse to accept them as 'words'.

In theory, the difference between a proper name and a common one is that the former refers to a set containing only one member, whereas the latter is a generic term denoting a whole category of similar members. The motive of word-gamers in rejecting names is that acquaintance with them is a test of general knowledge, whereas word games are intended to be a test of literacy. It is reasonable to expect word-gamers to have *mountain* in their vocabulary; it is not reasonable to expect them to know *Matterhorn* any more than *Makalu* or *Mercedario*.

In practice, of course, many names do not have unique referends. I am not the only *David* in the street, let alone the world. There could be as many *Davids* as there are *dogs*, and it is reasonable to expect literate people to have both words in their vocabulary. Even so, a name is felt to be unique rather than generic, as may be gauged by the incongruous effect produced by assuming the opposite in the following encounter from *The Lost Weekend*:

Hospital orderly Name?
Ray Milland Birnam.
Orderly What kind of a Birnam?
Milland DON Birnam.

Proper names are shared only because there are not enough of them to go around. *Dog* is generic because it will do for any individual member of a genus of animals which we are all capable of recognizing; we could not look at a person and know for certain that it was a *Birnam* or a *David*.

At first sight, English appears to help word-gamers by its convention of writing names with capital initials. Even more advantageously, names which become used as generics drop their capitals. Thus *moll*, originally a proper name (diminutive of Mary), comes to mean a gangster's girl-friend, in which capacity it takes a small M and is acceptable as a generic word or common noun. Similarly, *quisling* is now acceptable as a common-noun synonym for 'traitor', and *boycott* is a verb. (More surprisingly, *guy* is from Fawkes and *gun* from Gunhilda.)

Unfortunately, this is not always the case. We may refer to a poet as a Shakespeare or a Byron, but not with a small S or B. It all comes down to a question of whether or not we *feel* certain names to be 'proper' in any given circumstance. Once again, we trip over the line that can't be drawn.

More serious, because unnoticed by many players, English happens to use capital initials for words whose status as 'proper' names is highly questionable. What about days of the week and months of the year? I regard Sunday, January, Monday, February and the rest as generics and favour the French custom of spelling them with small initials. Yet so deeply ingrained is the contrary behaviour of the English that I have even been challenged for spelling the four seasons with small letters instead of capitals!

Again, what about nationals? The French, bless their logical minds, quite properly spell their words for *Frenchman*, *Icelander* and so on with a small initial. It seems obvious to me that Frenchmen are generic rather than proper. The same applies to languages, though with less force: I can see the argument behind treating *French* as a proper name, insofar as it denotes a unique language. Less defensible is our habit of spelling adjectives of nationality with a capital initial, except in given phrases. What is the difference between a 'French widow' and a 'french window'? Not just the N in window, but the F in French as well.

Many word-gamers also disallow the so-called 'names' of letters of the alphabet. To my mind, one aitch is as generic as another. Nobody insists that they be spelt with capital initials, but that doesn't stop them from banning the words. And if names of English letters are prohibited, what about Greek and Hebrew? If *pi* is acceptable because, besides being a Greek letter, it denotes a mathematical quantity, is not the Hebrew *aleph* precisely analogous to the extent that it denotes an order of infinity. Are *el* and *es* more 'proper' than *six* and *seven*?

Problems of consistency can arise with names of plants and animals. All creatures great and small have scientific names, great and small, taken mainly from Latin. Whereas no one would object to *wolf* in a word game, neither part of its scientific name, *Canis lupus*, would be accepted, the former if only because it is (by international convention) spelt with a capital, the latter if only because it is Latin and therefore 'foreign'. There is no problem here because we have a so-called popular word (*wolf*), which is quite distinct from the scientific. But problems can arise where no popular word exists. *Dinosaur* has long been a popular word and was never very scientific in the first place, but word-gamers may quite naturally balk at *Stegosaurus* or *Triceratops*. Strictly speaking, or writing, they are spelt with capitals; whether or not they should be so spelt in popular writings is an open question. I pose the question only to be awkward, not to answer it, though I dare say most players would agree with me in accepting them on an equal footing with *dog* and *wolf*.

The gist of my argument, in case it has got lost in the under-growth, is that proper names should not be allowed in word games because they belong to specialized knowledge rather than to literacy. The task of deciding which names are proper and which generic, or common, is too elaborate for practical play. It is therefore a poor best to prohibit words which in English are only spelt with a capital initial, even if this means throwing out with the specific bathwater such generic babies as Monday, Zed and Tyrannosaurus rex.

I leave this subject with a few names of ponderable propriety. What about: *Londoner? Mancunian? Petrine* (epistles)? *Caesar? Mackintosh? Ford? Formica? Spa? Lido? Thermos?*

And did you know that the plural of THERMOS is THERMOI?

Foreign Words Talking of thermoses reminds me that of all the restrictions commonly followed in word games none is more laudable than the prohibition of foreign words, smelling as they do of goat-skins, cheap wine and garlic. English speakers rightly take it for granted that the game is to be played in English: if foreign words are allowed an unfair advantage accrues to the most accomplished linguist among them.

Unfortunately, though laudable, the rule is unenforceable. There is a line, again, that won't be drawn.

The problem arises because English has a habit of picking up foreign words and gradually absorbing them into its lexicon until a point is reached at which they cease to sound foreign. They are then not foreign but only of foreign origin. By this process, more English words actually turn out to be foreign than native: it has often been pointed out that English is a Germanic language with a vocabulary of which some seventy-five per cent is Romance (ultimately derived from Latin).

It is aggravated by the fact that no two dictionaries, and often no two players, will agree on the extent to which a word in question has become naturalized. The *Oxford English Dictionary* attaches a sign to words not regarded as naturalized, but as it was compiled over a century ago this is not very helpful.

English easily absorbs foreign words for both phonetic and syntactic reasons. It has a large, rich sound system which can accommodate almost any foreign word with a fair approximation to its original sound – although, in practice, English speakers have a notorious tendency to anglicize beyond recognition. An interesting example of phonetic flexibility is the English speaker's readiness to reproduce passably the sound of CH in LOCH or GH in VAN GOGH, even though the sound dropped out of English itself several centuries ago. And the fact that English makes minimal use of grammatical modifications such as case-endings means that the absorption of foreign words is not hindered by problems of declension or conjugation.

Being, therefore, in a position to employ foreign words more or less indiscriminately, English readily does so in several different ways.

(1) Unlike the Romans, whose pains to translate everything into Latin extended even to the translation of Celtic gods into Mars, Apollo and so on, English-speakers quite happily retain native words for things peculiar to their country of origin. Thus, for the price of one *zloty* you may drink *slivovitz* while playing the *crwth* in a *troika*. *Olé!*

(2) English-speakers will often not trouble to find equivalents for words denoting things of foreign invention, albeit of international applicability. Hence, the pen of my *ombudsman* is in the *bidet*.

(3) Even where an English synonym exists, the native word may be retained for greater accuracy or local colour. Both *pueblo* and *kampong* can be replaced by 'village', but this does not prevent them from being listed in *Chambers*. An interesting tailpiece to this observation is the use of the native spelling *cwm* for such a 'coomb' as may be found in Wales, from which the name was borrowed and anglicized in the first place.

(4) Foreign words are often retained for abstractions where, again, the use of English equivalents may lose in the translation. *Apartheid* is likelier to lead to *angst* than to *détente*.

(5) If the three words just quoted are used as much for emotional colouring as for accuracy, others are employed for accuracy without the slightest taint of emotive connotation. Such are mainly technical terms, largely from Greek and Latin, with examples rife in biology and medicine: *rubella*, *sinus*, the genus *Homo*. It is interesting to note that *Chambers* lists *manus* for 'hand' but not *pes* for 'foot', though both may be encountered in the same context. To this category belong also Italian musical terms such as *allegro*, *crescendo*, and *niente*.

All the foreign words quoted above are, to my mind,

acceptable as English in word games, and I should like to think that most players would agree. At the same time, I cannot believe that any self-respecting word-gamer would accept the German *Gesellschaft* for 'company' (commercial), even though it is listed in *Chambers*.

On the whole, I have a fairly liberal attitude towards foreign words. I tend to accept a word unless the dictionary specifically describes it as foreign or ascribes it to a foreign language other than to indicate its origin. Doubtful cases may be tested by asking the claimant word-maker to propose a sentence or context in which the foreign word would be the natural choice of an educated English-speaker.

As a postscript, I do object to the use of individual foreign words abstracted from phrases or sayings. Neither *desperandum* from 'nil desperandum', nor *cul* from 'cul-de-sac', nor *sturm* from 'Sturm und Drang', nor *istesso* from 'l'istesso tempo', nor *hoi* from 'hoi polloi' has independent existence as a word in English contexts; they should be disallowed for that reason.

Dialectical words Most word-gamers quite properly do not count dialectal variants of English as 'foreign' and consequently allow dialectical words as valid. But few go so far as to discuss the point, which I think is a little short-sighted as there are various pitfalls which can lead to argument. The matter is not helped by the fact that, although everyone knows more or less what they mean by 'dialect', there is no precise linguistic definition of it. The term is often employed patronizingly out of ignorance. I recently read that a WANTED FOR MURDER poster circulated in England appeared not only in English but also in the Indian 'dialects' of Urdu, Punjabi and Gujerati. The writer of the book evidently assumed that different languages, if spoken in the same state, are dialects of one. This argument would make Welsh and Gaelic dialects of English, which, of course, they aren't.

Dialect is not a strong term amongst the English because regional varieties of the notional 'standard' vary little from one another compared with those of more strongly differentiated languages such as Italian. The only English dialect sufficiently well marked to boast literary status is Lallans or Lowlands (Scots). (It is sufficiently marked to be discussable as a language. A Dutch friend of mine once reported that he switched on the radio one Sunday morning to hear what he thought was a church service conducted in Frisian. It turned out to be Lallans.) A goodly proportion of the words in many English dictionaries are designated 'Scots', and, although I do not necessarily disagree with their acceptance, I am surprised not to have read any *questioning* of their allowability in books and articles on English word-gaming. Should Sassenach word-gamers be expected to know such words as *kye* for 'cows', *fley* for 'frighten', *sark* for 'shirt' – for any purpose, that is, other than to show them off in word games? And if these, which appear in *Chambers*, what about those that do not: *mebbies* for 'perhaps', *inower* (a compound preposition), *throuither* for 'jumbled up'?

British word-gamers south of the border may be forgiven for their greater knowledge of American English than of Scots. The general meaninglessness of the word 'dialect' may be indicated by noting that, to Britishers, American is a dialect as opposed to a standard, while, to Americans, British is equally a dialect. It is interesting to note that British players will generally accept American words as valid (*movie*, *debunk*, *racketeer*, etc.) but not American spellings of words common to both languages (*harbor*, *kilometer*, *defense*). At least, literate people such as word-gamers do not. Professional illiterates such as journalists and sociologists tend to use American spelling as much as American vocabulary, probably without noticing it.

In the British National Scrabble Championship rules, I have just noticed, words listed in *Chambers* only as 'US', such as *bronco*, are disallowed as being foreign. I find this extraordinary, in view of the unquestioning acceptance of vocabulary listed only as 'Scots'!

Obsolete, obsolescent and archaic words and spellings It is a commonplace of knowledge that languages evolve, losing and acquiring new vocabulary and undergoing shifts and drifts of grammatical structure. We have already commented on the gradual absorption of words which start out as foreign and gradually become so naturalized that the discovery of their origin comes as a surprise.

In counterpoint to the absorption of new vocabulary runs the gradual shedding of the old. When a word ceases to be current it has started on the road of obsolescence: it becomes first quaint, then old-fashioned, then archaic, and finally obsolete. These are not precise terms, of course; the process is more gradual than their use implies.

The general practice of word-gamers is to prohibit words which have reached the final stage and are accordingly marked 'obs.' in the dictionary. As to archaic words, such as *thee* and *thou*, surviving only in specialized contexts, lips may be pursed and acceptance grudgingly granted. Fair enough; but then problems arise with the appropriate verb forms. If *thou* is permitted, so must be *hast*; if *hast*, why not also *hath*, *seeth* and *wert*? Where is the line to be drawn?

Care must be taken not to dismiss words as obsolete or archaic merely because the thing they refer to has vanished from the scene. Groats are obsolete, but *groat* is not. The word remains current to the extent that it has not been replaced by a modern word for the same coin: you may yet dig one up in the garden and will know exactly what to call it. Granted, you are more likely to unearth a sixpence or a shilling, but the same principle applies. In similar vein, mermaids and unicorns may not exist, but *mermaid* and *unicorn* undoubtedly do.

The same might be argued of words listed only as Shakespearian or, worse still, Spenserian – but not by me. Personally, I reject them as obsolete. This may be challenged as inconsistent with the argument supporting groats and unicorns; but was it not somebody-or-other who once said that 'Consistency is the bugaboo of petty minds'?

Obsolete spellings are more easily dealt with – i.e. rejected – on the ground that no literate person would use them in preference to the modern spelling. It should be noted, however, that some words have equally common variant spellings, such as (*window-*)*sill* and *cill*. If the main entry in a dictionary quotes alternative spellings they are generally accepted by word-gamers, and there seems nothing wrong in that.

Slang, colloquialisms and 'familiar' words Some word-gamers prohibit slang, presumably on grounds of propriety. I don't object to current slang as such, but, as a parent, I do have sympathy with the view that children should be protected from foul language in the home. It is true that the foulness of some slang lies not in the words themselves but in the attitude of the speaker who uses them; but, again, it is an attitude of aggression and lack of self-control which children should not be allowed to emulate. Adult word-gamers may be able to employ such emotive terms with the clinical detachment of the linguist, but to admit them to children is akin to putting a gun in their hands.

The other reason for prohibiting slang, colloquialisms and the like is that they tend to be too ephemeral for inclusion in the dictionary, which is why nearly all dictionary words designated 'slang' seem so quaint and out of date. The reason is only valid if strict adherence to the dictionary is regarded as a rule of the game. I see no reason to prohibit words known to everybody merely because they are too ephemeral to be listed. This problem is overcome by my rule of appeal to other players.

Technical terms I wonder how long it will be before the computer word *byte* ceases to be technical and acquires metaphorical value in everyday use? There is no reason to ban technical terms, even if not listed by the dictionary, provided that their existence can be proved or at least one other player acknowledges a claim. Their situation is, in fact, similar to that of slang words and colloquialisms. Note that words designated 'foreign' in the dictionary may often be used in a technical sense – indeed, it is unlikely that they would otherwise be listed.

Abbreviations and acronyms I have met word-gamers who object to *bus* and *phone* on the ground that they are abbreviations and should be preceded by an apostrophe, and I once exchanged argument with a publisher (not Penguin) whose copy-editor disinfected my use of *ad* by soaking it in inverted commas. In principle, no objection can be made to abbreviations in everyday use. In pract, howev, the princ is ope to abuse. You have no choice but either to put it to the vote or to see how it is listed and described by the dictionary.

It may be helpful to draw a distinction between oral contractions and written abbreviations. No objection can reasonably be raised against such natural spoken contractions as *bus*, *phone*, *ad* and so on. That they are derived from longer words is just a matter of history. Many words in use today have similar backgrounds, which their users are quite unaware of. It would be as pedantic to object to *bus* from *omnibus* as it would to reject *mob* on the grounds that it derives by contraction from the two-word Latin phrase *mobile vulgus*. Written abbreviations, however, are merely orthographic conventions for words which are still normally pronounced in full, such as *Mr* for *mister*, *Ms* for *manuscript* and *St* for either *saint* or *street*. Abbreviations of this sort are clearly not allowable.

There are, inevitably, awkward borderline cases where pronunciation may follow orthographic abbreviation. For instance, the British National Scrabble Championship law-givers have recently accepted the word *viz*, a printer's conventional abbreviation of the Latin *videlicet*. Since what started as a purely orthographic convention has become 'live' in many speakers' mouths, I welcome the acceptance. Unfortunately, none of the other members of my word-gaming circle have ever allowed me to count it.

We live in an age of acronyms. The anti-smoking lobby in Britain calls itself Action on Smoking and Health in order to secure for itself the appropriate acronym A S H, which strikes me as rather more successful than S I G M A for the Society of Inventors of Games and Mathematical Attractions. Examples of words that originated as acronyms include *posh* (Port Out, Starboard Home, according to the generally accepted explanation), *radar* (R Adio Detection And Ranging – note the additional appropriateness of the palindrome) and *laser* (Light Amplification by Stimulated Emission of Radiation). Will LEM (Lunar Excursion Module) follow in their wake? Try using it in a word game and see. I would not object to it, as it bears all the hallmarks of a pronounceable English word – which is more than can be said for VTOL (Vertical Take-Off and Landing). Had they called it VERTAKOL, or even VERKOL, word-gamers would probably have found it acceptable.

In deciding whether or not to accept a claimed acronym as a word, it seems reasonable to apply two tests. First, is it generic or specific? UNESCO is essentially a name, therefore unacceptable if names are prohibited (as I believe they should be), whereas LEM could refer to any old lunar lander and for that reason is generic enough to be accepted. Second, does it make an unambiguously pronounceable word according to the (admittedly somewhat haphazard) rules of English orthography? LEM is also acceptable by this test, but VTOL is not: VT never occurs at the front of an English word, and readers would vary in their pronunciation according to the vowel sound they insert between the two consonants. I would accept an acronym that passes both tests.

Hyphenated and compound words A compound word is made when two or more are stuck together to make a whole which means more than the sum of its parts: a workshop is a place where a craft is carried out and would not do for the local shop where local shop-assistants work. The trouble with English is that we hyphenate some such compounds and not others. No player would object to *workshop* as a word claimed in a game, but I doubt if any would accept *shopassistant*. The artificiality involved in sticking words together or keeping them separate may be demonstrated by a phrase such as State Security Head Office, which is a word-for-word translation of the c.1939 German *Reichssicherheitshauptamt*. Word games tend to be tests of the written language, and what is or is not acceptable has nothing to do with sense or logic, only with form and convention. The Germans write their compounds as one word; we tend to keep them apart unless this leads to misunderstanding.

British word-players also suffer from hyphens, a disease from which the Americans are comparatively free. Even where compounds are regarded as greater than the sum of their parts, the English generally prefer to keep them at a hyphen's length apart. To add to the confusion, the hyphen is also a piece of punctuation rather than an integral part of the spelling, and may be inserted or omitted according to the sense – a *well-known* fact that may not be as *well known* as it appears.

As Sir Ernest Gowers puts it in *The Complete Plain Words*, 'If you take hyphens seriously you will surely go mad.'

In British English we stress the noun rather than the adjective preceding it, as in *red* CABbage and *red* ADmiral. When such word pairs become more closely linked in a perhaps metaphorical sense, we may go so far as to hyphenate them in writing without altering the stressed syllable in speech, as in *red-*BLOODed or *red-*HANDed. Eventually, however, we so far regard the pair as forming a unit as to transfer the stress to the adjective before it as if the whole thing were a single noun, as in RED-*belly* and RED-*head*. A final stage of coalescence is reached when the hyphen is dropped from the written word, as in REDskin and REDcurrant. (Similar remarks apply to other word pairs such as noun-noun, object-verb and so on.) Looked at in this way, the presence of a hyphen in a compound may suggest that the words involved are undergoing a process of evolution into one.

Here are some further examples (hyphenation etc. follows *Chambers* in all cases):

Stage 1	*Stage 2*	*Stage 3*	*Stage 4*
Long ODDS	Long-WINDed	LONG-hand	LONGbow
Under AGE	Under-PRIvileged	UNder-trick	UNderdog
House RULES	House-SURgeon	HOUSE-leek	HOUSEhold
Iron LUNG	Iron-GREY	IRon-mine	IRonstone
Round OFF	Round-TAble	ROUND-up	ROUNdhead

In British word play, stage 1 compounds would certainly not be accepted, those at stage 4 certainly would be. Most would also disallow all those written with hyphens, although, on appeal from a claimant, I would allow those which either I or the dictionary regard as belonging to stage 3.

This is one way of attacking the problem, but, of course, it is much too awkward for average word play. Prohibiting hyphenated words without examination is a practical necessity rather than a desirable ideal.

Americans do not have this problem, since the tendency of the language is to throw the stress back to the adjective or attributive regardless. 'He's a crazy man,' pronounced by an American, sounds as if *crazyman* is all one word. Hence, in American, word-pairs may bed down overnight without passing through the formality of a hyphen. Words which are still single in British but indissolubly spliced in American include alright ('all right' in British), *underway*, *anytime*, *anymore*, *worldwide* and nodoubtmanyothers.

Some words, though hyphenated for one reason or another, are so patently single words that, if it were up to me, I would allow them in word games. Examples include *X-ray*, *so-called*, *cul-de-sac*, *forget-me-not* and, especially, *co-operative* or *co-operation*. (If you must split them, says Gowers, use a diaeresis – that's what they're for. *Unco-operative* looks like a Scots expression. *Uncoöperative* is better, and *uncooperative* better still.)

Whether or not to allow words containing apostrophes, such as *fo'c'sle*, is a matter of taste. But no one, I think, would argue in favour of two-word contractions like *shan't*, *ain't* or *would've*.

Interjections   *Oh! Ah!* and *Eh?* are interjections recognized by *Chambers* and most word-gamers. *Chambers* also recognizes *Sh!* and *St!*, which some players would feel dubious about if only because they don't contain vowels, along with *Fy!* and *La!*, which cannot have been heard in real English speech for a long time now. It does not recognize *Aw!* for a characteristically American form of self-expression, or *Mm!* for delighted agreement, or the equally conventional *Zz!* indicating mid-snooze, or even the less arguable and self-explanatory *Ow!*

If your dictionary is as inconsistent as *Chambers* in its choice of interjections, you have several choices of action. One is to accept all interjections listed plus those accepted by at least one other opponent on appeal. Another is to ban all interjections, for which you would have my support. Yet a third would be to ban all two-letter words from word games and so dispense with almost the entire problem. That is my preferred solution.

Names also usable as generic words

Many words which may be disallowed from word games because they are chiefly known as names have, nevertheless, a generic meaning or usage for which a capital initial is not required.

The following is a list of names which are also acceptable with a small letter as game words. They are chiefly, but not exclusively, personal forenames. Others are family or place names. Deliberately omitted are names which are too well known as common words to need listing; for example, female and flower names such as *pansy*, *heather*, *violet*, etc.

ABIGAIL
ABRAM (obs.)
ALEXANDERS (pl. only)
ALEXANDRINE
ALMA
AMAZON
AMELIA
ANN (Scot.)
ANNA
AVA
BARNEY
BASIL
BENEDICT
BENJAMIN
BERTHA
BERYL
BETTY
BIDDY
BILLY
BLANCH (without -E)
BOB(BY)
CAROL (without -E)
CECILS (pl. only)
CELESTE
CELESTINE
CHARLIE, -EY
CHARLOTTE
CHRISTIANA
CHRISTIE, -EY
CICELY
CLARENCE
CLEMENT(INE)

COLLIE
CRAIG (Scot.)
CRISPIN
DAVENPORT
DERRICK
DICK, -Y, -EY
DICKENS
EBENEZER
EMMA
ERIC (but not -A)
FANNY (slang)
FAY
FLORA
FLOSSY (but not -IE)
FRENCH
GEMMA
GENE
GEORGETTE
GLORIA (Latin)
GREGORY
HARRY
HENRY
HOMER
INGRAM (obs.)
IRIS
ISABEL(-LA), not ISO-
JACK
JAMES
JANE
JEAN
JAPAN
JASMINE
JEFF
JEMIMA
JEMMY
JENNY*
JEREBOAM

JERRY
JERSEY
JESS
JILL
JIMMY (US, not UK)
JO
JOANNA
JOBE
JOEY
JO(H)ANNES
JOHN (US, not UK)
JOSS
JUD
JUDAS
JUDY
JULIENNE
JUVENAL
KELVIN
KEN
KITTY
LAMBERT
LAURA
LEWIS
LILL (Scot.)
LIONEL
LOUIS
MADGE
MAG
MADRAS
MAGDALEN(E)
MARGARITE
MARGUERITE
MARTIN
MAUD
MAVIS
MAXWELL
MAY

MICK(-EY, -Y)
MIKE
MINA
MOLL(Y)
MONA
MUNGO
MYRTLE
NANCY
NANNY
NEDDY
NELLY
NGAIO
NORMA
NORMAN
OLIVER
OTTO
PADDY
PAM
PATTY
PAUL
PEGGY
PEREGRINE
PERRY
PETER
POLL(Y)
REGINA

REX*
REYNARD
ROGER*
RORY
ROSEMARY
RUTH
SALLY
SAUL (Scot.)
SHEILA
SOPHIA (not -IE)
STEPHANE
STEPNEY
TALBOT
TIMON (obs.)
TIMOTHY
TOBY
TOM(MY)
TONY (obs. slang)
VALENTINE
VALERIAN
VERONICA
VESTA
VICTOR (not -IA)
WALLY
WELLINGTON
WILLY

* *Notes* The list was compiled by checking through *Chambers* headwords with concentration on personal forenames. The name *Constance* is proper only, though the *OED* records it as obsolete for 'constancy'. *Chambers* does not record *jenny*, *joanna* or *rex* without a capital initial – all of which I would accept – and is ambiguous about *roger*. However, the inadequacy of *Chambers* in this respect is demonstrated by its listing of *swede* only with a capital initial, even though no literate person would so spell the vegetable of that name. Some names, such as *Vanessa* (= the Red Admiral butterfly), cannot be spelt with a small initial even when not used personally, since, under the international system of taxonomic nomenclature, a generic name (i.e. that of a genus) always has a capital, and a specific (that of the species) usually a small initial. This should not, however, debar names of genera for which the scientific and popular words are identical, such as *pteranodon* and the like.

Two-letter Words

Here is a list of two-letter words which may be claimed but not necessarily accepted in word games. It is not intended to be helpful, but rather to support the argument that all two-letter words should be banned. Dictionaries are generally inconsistent as to which they include or omit, and it is either a gamble or a question of list-memorization as to whether or not a claimed word will be supported by the dictionary referred to.

Players are recommended to accept or reject whole classes of words rather than individuals. If one sol-fa note is allowed, all should be; if one letter of the Greek alphabet, then all letters of Greek and Roman alphabets.

All words listed here appear in the *Oxford English Dictionary* unless otherwise marked, except for most elements of the tonic sol-fa system, which are taken in their entirety (including sharps and flats) from *Grove's Dictionary of Music*. The *OED* includes a few other words of two letters omitted from this list because designated obsolescent or abbreviated.

Word	Meaning or Function (when not in common use)	Possible Objection
AA	volcanic lava	not in *OED*
AD		not in *OED*
AE	one	dialectal
AF	of	dialectal
AH		interjection
AI	three-toed sloth	obscure
AM		–
AN		–
AR	the letter R	alphabetical
AS		–
AT		–
AW	*interjection*	interjection (*OED* says obsolete)
AX		unusual spelling in UK, preferred by *OED*
AY	yes; ever	–

BA	musical note	sol-fa
BE		–
BO	*interjection*	interjection
BY		–
CE	the letter C	alphabetical
CO	come	dialectal
DA	father; Burmese knife	obscure
DE	musical note	sol-fa
DO		–
DY	lake sediment	not in *OED*
EA	river	dialectal
EE	eye; *Lancashire interjection*	dialectal
EF	the letter F	alphabetical
EH		interjection
EL	the letter L	alphabetical
EM	printers' measure	specialized
EN	half an em	specialized
ER		interjection, not in *OED*
ES	the letter S	alphabetical
EX	person no longer of given status	not in *OED*
FA	musical note	sol-fà (but in *OED*)
FE	musical note	sol-fa
FU	musical note	sol-fa
FY		interjection
GO		–
GU	violin	obscure
HA		interjection
HE		–
HI		interjection
HM		interjection
HO	stop; *interjection*	obscure; interjection

ID		specialized (or obscure)
IE	pine tree	not in *OED*
IF		–
IN		–
IO	*interjection*	interjection
IS		–
IT		–
JO	darling	dialectal
KA	spirit	not in *OED*
KI	tropical tree	obscure
KO	term used in Go (game); *form of 'quoth'*	obscure
KY	cows	dialectal
LA	*interjection*; musical note	interjection; sol-fa (but in *OED*)
LI	Chinese unit of measurement	obscure
LO		interjection
LY	*variant of* LI	obscure
MA		–
ME		–
MI	musical note	sol-fa (but in *OED*)
MM	*interjection*	interjection
MO	more	dialectal
MU	letter of Greek alphabet	alphabetical, not in *OED*
MY		–
NA	no	dialectal
NE	*negative*	archaic
NO		–
NU	letter of Greek alphabet	alphabetical, not in *OED*
OB	objection	not in *OED*
OD	a hypothetical force	obscure
OE	grandchild	dialectal
OF		–

OH		interjection
OI	*interjection*	interjection, not in *OED*
OM	Hindu chant	not in *OED*
ON		–
OO	*interjection*	interjection
OR		–
OS	bone	obscure
OU	*interjection*	interjection, unusual spelling
OW	*interjection*	interjection
OX		–
OY	*form of* OE	dialectal
PA		–
PI		–
PO	chamber-pot	not in *OED* (or *Chambers*)
RA	musical note	sol-fa
RE	concerning; musical note	–
SA	musical note	sol-fa
SE	musical note	sol-fa
SH		interjection
SI	musical note	sol-fa, but in *OED*
SO		–
ST	*interjection*	interjection
SU	she	dialectal
TA	*interjection*	interjection
TE	musical note	sol-fa
TI	tree	obscure
TO		–
TY	musical note	sol-fa
UG	*expression of loathing*	dialectal
UH	*interjection*	interjection
UM	*interjection*	interjection
UN	one	dialectal
UP		–

UR	*interjection*	interjection
US		–
UT	musical note	sol-fa, but in *O E D*
UZ	us	dialectal
WA	interjection	dialectal interjection (!)
WE		–
WO	*interjection; variant of 'woe'*	interjection; obscure
XI	letter of Greek alphabet; numeral	not in *O E D*
XU	Vietnamese coin	not in OED
YE		archaic
YI	Chinese philosophical term	not in *O E D*
YO	*interjection*	interjection
YU	precious jade	not in *O E D*
ZO	Himalayan cattle breed	not in *O E D*
ZZ	*representation of slumber*	not in *O E D*

A total of 124, of which 30 may be regarded as acceptable without argument. There may be others.

Some useful statistics for word-gamers

Frequency of Occurrence of Letters in English .Words (per 1,000 letters)

In text		In dictionary	
E	131	E	109
T	105	A	91
A	82	I	78
O	80	R	75
N	71	T	72
R	68	O	69
I	63	N	62
S	61	L	61
H	53	S	58
D	38	C	49
L	34	U	37
F	29	P	34
C	28	D	32
M	25	M	30
U	25	H	28
G	20	G	23
Y	20	B	21
P	20	Y	19
W	15	F	14
B	14	V	10
V	9	W	10
K	4	K	9
X	2	X	3
J	1	Z	2
Q	1	Q	2
Z	1	J	2

Figures in the first list (from a book on codes and ciphers called *Secret and Urgent*) indicate with what relative frequency the letters of English occur in actual usage, e.g. messages or literature. In use, letter frequencies are affected by word frequencies. For example, T, H and E are made higher by the fact that *the* is one of the commonest words, as are *there*, *then*, *he*, etc.

Those in the second list (from computer-aided research carried out by the author) refer to letter frequencies of words as listed in the dictionary, i.e. once each. This is more useful to word-gamers, though most writers on word games mean text frequencies when they refer to frequency at all.

Relative Frequency of Letters as Initials and Finals

Initials SPCAM TBRDF HEIWG LOUNV KJQYZX
Finals   SETYN LRDCA HMGPO KFWBX IUZJQV

These refer to dictionary-listed words rather than running text. Although S is less common than D as the last letter of a word, it becomes the commonest final letter if grammatical uses are taken into account, i.e. plurals, possessives and third person verb endings. Since plurals, etc. are usually allowed in word games, S has here been shifted to first position. By my estimate, some 60 to 70 per cent of words can take an S ending for one reason or another.

Combinability of Letters

E is the most combinable letter, since it can be preceded or followed by almost any other. Q is low on the list, as it is only ever followed by U and can be preceded by few other letters. The order of letters from highest to lowest degree of combinability is roughly as follows:

EIAOR UTLSC PNDMG BHFYV WKQXZJ

The most commonly found pairs of consonants are:

ST, NT, TR, CH, LL, ND, TH, NG, BL, NC, SS, PR,
SH, CT, CK, PH, SC, RT, PL, NS, MP, SP, GR, SM,
TT, RD, CL, RR, RC, DR, RS, RN, FF, MB, RM,
GH, LD, DL.

These all occur with above-average frequency, ST being commonest and DL just about average. (Plurals and other words with added S were not included in the survey.)

The commonest diphthongs are:

OU, EA, IO, IA, OO, EE, AI, IE, UE, AU, EO, OI,
OW, UA.

(IO is commoner than might be expected because of words ending in -TION.)

Words Whose Only Vowel is 'Y'

Rules of word games and competitions are often spoilt by confusion over the status of the letter Y, which, because it is technically described as a semi-vowel, is regarded by most people as a consonant. This is nonsense. Y is merely a written variation of I, which is clearly a vowel, and is only a semi-vowel at the start of a syllable when followed by a different vowel (as in *yes*, *yam* and *yoyo*). According to my calculations, Y is used as a full vowel in about 97 per cent of all occurrences. It is obviously a vowel in the following words, which contain no other:

List of words containing Y as their only vowel

BY	FY	LYNCH
CRY	FYRD	LYNX
CRYPT	GYM	MY
CYST	GYP	MYRRH
DRY	GYPSY	MYTH
DY	HYMN	NYMPH
FLY	LY	PLY
FRY	LYMPH	PRY

PYGMY	SPY	TY
PYX	STY	WHY
RHYTHM	SYLPH	WRY
SHY	SYZYGY	WRYLY
SHYLY	THY	WYCH
SKY	THYMY	WYND
SLY	TRY	
SLYLY	TRYST	

Total: 46

Not recorded in the *O E D* are *dy*, a type of lake sediment, and *ty*, part of the full-blown version of the tonic sol-fa system, as confirmed by reference to *Grove's Dictionary of Music*. Doubts may be expressed about *fy*, an interjection which I would now describe as obsolete, and *ly*, recorded from one example only as a variant spelling of 'li', a Chinese measurement. Dialectical words can extend the list further.

Solutions to Problems

Superghost (p. 66)

PTAG is a ghost of HEPTAGON

Ultraghost (p. 69)

AGUE, BEVY, CAJOLERY, DOING, ELBOW, FEOFF, GARLIC, HELM, IVORY, JUXTAPOSE, KNOWN, LUNCH, MATRIX, NIGH, ORIGAMI, POLO, QUALM, RUSTIC, SYRUP, TWELFTH, UNWED, VAGUE, WHOM, XYLOPHONE, YTTRIUM, ZEALOT.

Beheadings (p. 92)

the original American list is:

ATYPICAL = 7	MEAGERNESS = 9
BRIGHTNESS = 9	NEVERMORE = 8
CHASTEN = 6	OROTUND = 6
DEVOLUTION = 9	PRESIDENTIAL = 11
EVALUATION = 9	REVOLUTIONARY = 12
FRIGHTFULLY = 10	SPECULATION = 10
GASTRONOMICAL = 12	TREASONABLE = 10
HARBOR = 5	UPRAISE = 6
ISLANDER = 7	VINDICATION = 10
JUNCTION = 7	WHEREABOUTS = 10
KNIGHTLY = 7	YOURSELVES = 9
LITERATE = 7	ZONE = 3

Total: 199.

In British English, HARBOUR and ARBOUR are spelt with a U, adding one to the total, and there is no such word as MEAGER-NESS or EAGRESS. For the same length, an entry for M would be MATHEMATIC.

Acrosticals (p. 103)

Highest-scoring words from CUSTOMABLE were CALU-METS 8, UMBELS 6, STUMBLE 7, TUMBLES 7, OSCULATE 8, MUSCLE 6, ALMOST 6, BECALMS 7, LOCUST 6, ELMS 4, total 65.

PNEUMATICS yielded PANTIES 7, NICEST 6, EN-CAMPS 7, UNTIES 6, MANTIS 6, AUNTIES 7, TEACUPS 7, INMATES 7, CATNIP 6, SEMANTIC 8, total 67.

CENTRALITY produced CERTAINTY 9, ENTRAIL 7, NATTILY 7, TERTIAL 7, REALITY 7, ARTICLE 7, LITERACY 8 (mis-spelt with double T by one of the players!), INTERACT 8, TENACITY 8, YTTRIC 6 (an adjective deduced from 'yttrium' and happily confirmed by *Chambers*), total 74.

In several cases there are alternative words of the same length.

Oilers (p. 118)

It will come as no surprise to mathematical games-players that the first to move can always win with correct play, whether he is the toiler or the spoiler in this instance.

Constructapo (p. 123)

It's a long road over the mountain
   And my shoes are fallen to bits,
And I hear folk saying my singing
   Has gone the way of my wits.

(From 'The Song of the Old Fiddler' in *Dermot O'Byrne: Selected Poems of Arnold Bax*, edited by Lewis Foreman, by permission of the Bax Estate and Thames Publishing. Copyright © The Bax Estate, 1979)

Fictionary Dictionary (pp. 167–8)

CRITH = a unit of mass
EYRA = a South American wild cat
MAMMEE = a West Indian fruit
PROG = to poke about, forage, etc.
ZOSTER = an ancient Greek belt

Encyclopedia Fictannica (pp. 171–2)

LEVANT ET COUCHANT refers to the legal right to restrain cattle.

Whose Who's Who? (pp. 172–3)

ROSA BONHEUR was the French animal-painter.

Blind Dates (p. 173)

In 1493 the Songhai Empire really was brought to the height of its prestige.

Suspended Sentences (p. 177)

H E O T H O T F M = He entered on the history of the friendly move.

Jotto (p. 184)

Five such words supported by *Chambers* are CHUNK, FJORD, GYMPS, VIBEX, WALTZ, and five by Webster's are FUDGY, JAMBS, PHLOX, QUINT, WRECK (Source: Ross Eckler).

Bibliography

This is a list of books and other sources which I found useful or suggestive in the compilation of this one, and to whose authors I therefore gladly acknowledge indebtedness.

ANON *Cassells Book of In-Door Amusements, Card Games and Fireside Fun* (Cassell, London, 1881; facsimile edition, 1973; also incorporated into *Cassell's Book of Sport and Pastimes*, 1893)

BLOOMFIELD, LEONARD *Language* (Allen & Unwin, London, 1933)

BRANDRETH, GYLES *Indoor Games* (Hodder & Stoughton, London, 1977)

— *The Complete Book of Scrabble* (Robert Hale, London, 1980)

— *Pears Book of Words* (Pelham, London, 1979)

DIACK, HUNTER *Test Your Own Wordpower* (Paladin, St Albans, 1975)

ESPY, WILLARD R. *The Game of Words* (Wolfe, London, 1971)

FIXX, JAMES F. *Games for the Superintelligent* (Muller, London, 1977)

— *More Games for the Superintelligent* (as above)

GARDNER, MARTIN *The Annotated Alice* (Penguin, Harmondsworth, 1965)

MCCALLUM, GEORGE P. *101 Word Games (for Students of English as a Second or Foreign Language)* (Oxford University Press, New York, 1980)

MORRIS, WILLIAM and MARY *The Word Game Book* (Penguin, New York, 1975)

PENNYCOOK, ANDREW *The Indoor Games Book* (Faber and Faber, London, 1973)

PRATT, FLETCHER *Secret and Urgent* (Blue Ribbon, New York, 1939)

SACKSON, SID *A Gamut of Games* (Nelson, London, 1974)

SHARP, RICHARD *The Best Games People Play* (Ward Lock, London, 1976)

Reference books

I have browsed through many dictionaries while working on this book but cannot recommend any of them as being especially suitable for serious word-gamers. Reference books referred to in the text are:

Chambers Twentieth Century Dictionary, ed. A. M. Macdonald (Chambers, Edinburgh, 1972. A completely revised edition was published in 1977.)
The Oxford English Dictionary (Oxford University Press, Oxford, 1979: compact edition of the complete text revised up to 1933)
Pears Cyclopaedia (published annually by Pelham, London)
The Penguin Encyclopedia of Places by W. G. Moore (Penguin, Harmondsworth, 1971)

Also useful are:

The Acronyms, Initialisms and Abbreviations Dictionary, ed. Ellen T. Crowley (Gale Research Company, Detroit, 1978)
Chambers Scots Dictionary, ed. Alexander Warrack (Chambers, Edinburgh, 1979; first published 1911)
Mrs Byrne's Dictionary of Unusual, Obscure and Preposterous Words, by Josepha H. Byrne (Granada, St Albans, 1978)
Webster's New World Dictionary, ed. David B. Geralnik (Collins, London, 1977)
Words for Crosswords and Word Games, ed. A. M. Macdonald (Chambers, Edinburgh, 1979: the words in *Chambers Twentieth Century Dictionary* listed without definitions)

Periodicals

The following will be of interest to word-gamers:

The Gamer (formerly *Games & Puzzles*, ed. David Pritchard (published two-monthly by A. H. C. Publications, 23a George Street, Luton, Bedfordshire)
The Logophile, ed. Jeremy Geelan (published quarterly by Logophile Press, 47–9 Caledonian Road, London, N1.)
Word Ways: The Journal of Recreational Linguistics, ed. A. Ross Eckler (published quarterly by A. Ross Eckler, Spring Valley Road, Morristown, New Jersey 07960)

Index of Games

Acronymia, 61
Acrosticals, 102
Ad Lib, 37
Adverbs, 31
Aesop's Mission, 79
Alphabent, 120
Alphabet Race = Alphacross, 131
Alphacross, 131
Anaghost, 66
Anagrams, 178
Arrow of Letters, 111
A-to-Z Banquet, 52

Backenforth, 77
Bacronyms, 89
Bananas, 28
Beheadings, 91
Bizz, 55
Black Squares, 147
Blind Dates, 173
Botticelli, 75
Buzz, 55

Captions Courageous, 174
Categories, 93
Centurion, 114
Charades, 47
Clue Words, 78
Consequences, 123
Constructapo, 122
Convergence, 186

Crambo, 59
Crash, 185
Crossword = Wordsworth, 140

Daft Definitions, 21
Defective Detective, 26
Dictionary = Acrosticals, 102
Dictionary Game = Fictionary
    Dictionary, 162, 163
Digrams, 85
Donkey = Ghost, 64
Double Cross, 130
Double Jeopardy, 185
Dumb Crambo, 45

Encyclopedia Fictannica, 171

Fabulary Vocabulary, 169
Fictionary Dictionary, 163
Fore and Aft, 88
Foreheads, 193
Free Association, 56

Game of the Name, 20
Get the Message, 191
Ghost, 64
Giotto = Jotto, 182
Guggenheim, 98

Hangman, 180
Headlines, 124
Heads and Tails, 58

Head to Tail, 89
He Who Hesitates = Ad Lib, 37
Hobby Horse, 29
Hypochondriac, 53

I Love My Love, 51
Inflation, 115
Initial Sentences = Acronymia, 61
Inquisition, 30
I Packed My Bag, 53
I Spy, 70

Jotto, 182
Just a Minute, 34

Key Word, 71
Key Words = Word Hunt, 99
Knock, Knock, Who's There?, 16
Kolodny's Game, 81

Last Word, 160
Last Word = Up the Dictionary, 62
Licence Plate Game = Ultraghost, 67
Life Sentence, 61
Lynx, 143

Mornington Crescent, 57

Name in Vain, 104
Number Plate Game = Ultraghost, 67
Numwords, 92
Nymphabet, 109

Oilers, 116
Oral Alphabent, 53
Orrible Origins, 22

Pass It On, 125
Phrase Maze = Get the Message, 191
Pi, 146
Prefixes, 87
Proverbs, 43

Quick Thinking, 29
Quizl, 187

Ragaman, 156
Railway Carriage Game, 32
Rhyme in Time = Crambo, 59
Roman Buzz, 55

Scorewords = Wordsworth, 140
Scramble, 133
Sequences, 90
Shaffe's Game, 78
Shouting Proverbs, 44
Silly Similes, 23
Sinko, 136
Spelling Bee, 39
Spelling Round, 40
Stairway, 91
Suffixes, 88
Superghost, 66
Suspended Sentences, 176

Taboo, 39
Target = Word Hunt, 99
Teapot, 27
Telegrams, 119
Tennis-Elbow-Foot Game, 56
Tom Swifties, 25
Tonto, 25
Trailers, 59
Travelling Alphabet, 52
Trigrams, 87
Twenty Questions, 72

Ultraghost, 67
Uncrash, 105
Up the Dictionary, 62

Verbal Sprouts = Arrow of
　Letters, 111
Vulture Up To?, 24

What Sort of Game am I?, 18
Who am I?, 75
Whose Who's Who?, 172

Wild Crash, 186
Word Hunt, 99
Word Ladder, 98
Wordnums = Numwords, 92
Word Ping-Pong, 107
Wordsquares = Wordsworth,
　140
Words within Words = Word
　Hunt, 99
Wordsworth, 140

Yessir, Nossir, 37

More About Penguins
and Pelicans

For further information about books available from Penguins please write to Dept EP, Penguin Books Ltd, Harmondsworth, Middlesex UB7 0DA.

In the U.S.A.: For a complete list of books available from Penguins in the United States write to Dept CS, Penguin Books, 625 Madison Avenue, New York, New York 10022.

In Canada: For a complete list of books available from Penguins in Canada write to Penguin Books Canada Ltd, 2801 John Street, Markham, Ontario L3R 1B4.

In Australia: For a complete list of books available from Penguins in Australia write to the Marketing Department, Penguin Books Australia Ltd, P.O. Box 257, Ringwood, Victoria 3134.

In New Zealand: For a complete list of books available from Penguins in New Zealand write to the Marketing Department, Penguin Books (N.Z.) Ltd, P.O. Box 4019, Auckland 10.

Tangram
The Ancient Chinese Shapes Game
Joost Elffers

Tangram, the 1000-year-old Chinese puzzle, is an exciting game which stimulates creativity and fantasy, and which can be played by one person or by a group.

The game consists of seven pieces, formed by cutting a square in a certain way, with which you can copy the examples given in this book. This may sound easy – but try it.

The Penguin Encyclopedia of Chess
Edited by Harry Golombek

A sumptuous work of reference, with entries covering every aspect of the game, from the theories and players to chess in the cinema and chess in Shakespeare.

'I prophesy that within only a few months chess-playing households throughout the English-speaking world, and indeed beyond it, will be seeking chess information, and settling chess arguments, with a cry of "Where's the Golombek?"' – Bernard Levin in *The Times*

More Games and Puzzles in Penguins

Mastering Rubik's Cube
Don Taylor

The bestselling guide to the twentieth-century's most perplexing puzzle, made clear by a world-famous Cube-master. Here Don Taylor takes you through the intricacies of the Cube so you'll be able to make patterns, play games, flip edges and twirl corners, create symmetry from chaos, break the three-minute barrier and – believe it or not – solve the Cube!

The Penguin Book of Card Games
David Parlett

From conventional Bridge and Poker to Klabberjass, Spite and Malice, Schafkopf and Bassadewitz, the 300 games are arranged in related groups, with an introduction to the pedigree and peculiarities of each family. More than seventy are described in detail, with hints on strategy and tricky points, while another 200 are concisely explained.

After all, as Talleyrand is supposed to have said: 'You can't play cards, young man? What a boring old age you're laying up for yourself!'